At the end of the Second World War, the people of Lancashire were trying to reassemble their lives. Many had been prisoners of war themselves and had lost friends and relatives during the fight against Germany. Rationing was still in force and times were hard for ordinary people. Yet the families of Oswaldtwistle welcomed German prisoners of war from the local camp into their homes at Christmas, and they later scraped together food and clothing to send to those same prisoners when they were repatriated to a devastated Germany.

Using letters, diaries and newspaper reports collected by her late father, Pamela Howe Taylor has uncovered a moving and little-known episode in our social history. The result is a story of compassion and humanity that will touch even the hardest of hearts.

Pamela Howe Taylor was born in 1939, the daughter of Rev. Joseph H. Howe, a Methodist minister. She spent most of her early childhood in Lancashire during which time the extraordinary and moving events described in this book took place. She has had a long and distinguished career in the Methodist Church and the Young Women's Christian Association, having held the posts of Methodist National Youth Secretary for World Affairs from 1973 to 1978, and YWCA North West Regional Secretary from 1978 to 1991. She and her husband now live in Devon, where she is Housing Officer for the YWCA in the West of England.

ENEMIES BECOME FRIENDS

A True Story of German Prisoners of War

Pamela Howe Taylor

The Book Guild Ltd
Sussex, England

The Book Guild Ltd.
25 High Street,
Lewes, Sussex

First published 1997
© Pamela Howe Taylor 1997
Reprinted 1998

Set in Times
Typesetting by Acorn Bookwork, Salisbury

Printed in Great Britain by
Bookcraft (Bath) Ltd, Avon

A catalogue record for this book is available from the British Library

ISBN 1 85776 189 8

Fig 1: In memory of my father, Rev. Joseph H. Howe 1900–1965

CONTENTS

Illustrations

THANKS AND ACKNOWLEDGEMENTS

Thanks are expressed to the people of Oswaldtwistle and the former prisoners of Stanhill Hostel. Special thanks to the many people named in this book and to other people who kindly and freely supplied information. In particular, acknowledgement is made for illustrations as follows:

Stanhill Camp site plan
Drawn by Koral Ahmet of the University of Manchester Archaeological Unit

Picture of German Prisoners' gift to Methodists
Methodist Recorder 12 December 1946

Photograph of Nissen hut
Courtesy of *Lancashire Evening Telegraph*

Photograph of Mount Pleasant Church
Mr E Yates

Photograph of Bruno Tietze on the poultry farm
Mr and Mrs Joseph Martin

Photograph of Heinz Hermann
Mrs S Duerden

Photographs of Fritz Herold, Werner Jungnichkel, Fred Haworth and others
Mr Fred Haworth

Picture of Mary Clark's Reunion
Mrs Mary Clark

FOREWORD
by Rev. Lord Soper

This is a true story of real people. It is at the same time a description in personal terms of one particular aspect of war. It is about German prisoners of war, a personal story of human relations as they are affected by war.

This, as a document, is a most valuable effort to understand and to communicate the nature of the arms struggle in this twentieth century.

Born in 1939, Pamela Taylor has pieced together the story of her father's ministry to German prisoners of war. It is his story of contact and friendship just after the end of the war with Germans in a neighbouring POW camp, and his concern and care for them and their families after repatriation in the conditions of near-starvation in post-war Germany.

I heartily recommend this meaning of Christian ministry. I am convinced that one of the most important and yet neglected elements in the whole barbarism and wickedness of war has been the way in which prisoners on both sides are witnesses to the argument that warfare itself is a crime. I have long been committed to the way of pacifism, as to, at one and the same time, the way of the Cross and the way to the Kingdom of God. The pages of this book are an eloquent testimony to the Christian Gospel of loving friend and foe in its understanding and practice.

INTRODUCTION

I was born six days after the Second World War started in 1939. My mother had missed the beginning of Sunday morning service on 3 September in order to listen to the wireless. As arranged, she then walked to church (in a very pregnant condition), up the aisle and into the pulpit to tell my father, the local Methodist minister, that Britain was at war. It fell to him to announce this dreaded news to the congregation.

I was too young to know much of the war itself. I do remember the heavy black material at every window, shortages of food and dress material, carrying a square box round my neck (my gas mask), the coupons needed to buy sweets, and the pictures of cream biscuits in the grocer's shop, which were never encountered in three dimensions. I can see the serried ranks of attentive men sitting on the left side of our church in Oswaldtwistle, Lancashire with names like Heinz and Ernst. Most of all I remember with excitement the wooden dolls' house given to me and my sister by the German prisoners. In a wartime childhood without elaborate toys it was a luxury.

After almost half a century, I started to piece together some old material of my late father's. Little by little a story emerged of these enemy prisoners of war in a camp on bleak moorland in Lancashire; a story of developing contact with local people, and of friendships which continued after the prisoners had returned to their unexpectedly deprived homeland. Some friendships have continued until this day.

This book tells an all-but-forgotten tale of ordinary people caught up in the aftermath of war, a war they probably never wanted in the first place.

1

Prisoners in Stanhill

It was May 1946, one year after the end of the war. I was in my second year of school at the age of six, travelling by bus and tram between the small Lancashire town of Oswaldtwistle and the larger town of Blackburn each morning and evening. The national milk scheme had just begun: at the mid-morning break from lessons we all sat at our desks drinking a third of a pint of milk through straws from the special-sized bottles.

Many things that we take for granted nowadays were unknown to us. We had never heard of television, fridges, washing machines, central heating, electric blankets, computers, supermarkets or motorways. There were no iron gates or railings to be seen anywhere. I remember being lifted up by my father to watch men taking the railings from the front garden of the house we had lived in prior to our move to Oswaldtwistle in 1944. Statistics say that 1,334,000 tons of metal had been collected in Britain by 1944 to be used for the manufacture of munitions.

Although my father was a Methodist minister travelling some miles each week to preach and visit members of his congregations (a very time-consuming part of his work), we never had a car. We had no electric equipment in the house at this time other than a telephone, light bulbs and an iron. Heating was by coal in open grates and all the manses we lived in had a coal shed in the back garden. The sound of shovelling of

3

coal was a familiar one. My father had a heavy manual type-writer and we relied on a large battery radio, positioned in the centre of the dining-room sideboard, for most of our news. Washing of clothes was done by hand with soap or soap flakes, using a corrugated wash-board and a hand-driven mangle. In our family we sent sheets and a few other items to a laundry which collected and delivered weekly. The unintelligible hoarse cry of the rag and bone man was heard in our streets, as he rode slowly by on his horse-drawn cart filled with scraps of worn-out belongings which people did not want but were reluctant to throw away.

Although the war was over, the effects of it were not. Most essential food was rationed and was to remain so for a further seven years. Ports had been main targets for bombing raids, so all imported food was very scarce. Each adult and child was allowed to purchase each week small quantities of meat, eggs, fat, sugar, cheese, bacon, milk, tea and sweets, if stocks and money permitted. A family registered with a grocer and butcher for each of these foodstuffs and then queued up for their rations each week, handing over the 'coupons' or 'points' cut out from the ration books. Many foods were not available at all and I was nine years old before I saw a banana.

In some respects Britain was not a comfortable place in 1946. Time spent in queues was a particular frustration. However, the threat of invasion had brought some measure of unity to the country and it was now at least realistic to hope for a better future.

Most people were probably unaware that the number of German prisoners in Britain was growing. Britain had become a stopping-place for prisoners on their way back home from prison camps in the USA and Canada. By the beginning of 1946 there were almost 200,000 such people; by May that year there were 338,000 and in September the number was given as 394,000. These prisoners were scattered throughout the country in over a thousand main camps and dependent hostels. As one writer put it, 'At the best of times the POW (prisoner of war) is in a difficult psychological situation, but a

4

POW on the side which has lost a calamitous war is beset with special difficulties... A few have not had news from their families for months. A sense of isolation and uncertainty regarding the future makes the POW apt to see things out of proportion.' (*Prisoners of War in Great Britain*, British Council of Churches pamphlet, April 1946.)

Of the 30 or so prisoner of war camps and hostels in the north west of England, one hostel was situated near Oswaldtwistle in Lancashire. The town is named after the seventh-century king of Northumbria, Oswald, and 'twistla' meaning a fork of land between two rivers. The area is known for its connection during the industrial revolution with two inventors. James Hargreaves, inventor of the 'spinning jenny' (named after his daughter), lived in Stanhill, Oswaldtwistle. The first Sir Robert Peel, textile printer and father of the future Prime Minister of the same name, was born at Peel Fold in Oswaldtwistle. He was known as 'Parsley' Peel because he used the parsley plant for his design.

The camp for prisoners was sited between Stanhill and Knuzden, small villages to the east of Blackburn surrounded by Lancashire moorland. It occupied a rectangular plot of land adjoining Stanhill Road, the B6234. An anti-aircraft station had been built during the war on the southern half of the field, with large gun emplacements to defend the armaments factories of the north west of England. In the northern half of the plot was the residential part of the camp. Italian prisoners were kept there during the latter part of the war but by 1946 all Italians who wanted to be repatriated had returned home. Now the camp housed German prisoners as a branch of Newton POW Camp 146, based in Kirkham near Preston. Stanhill Hostel, as it was officially known, consisted chiefly of rows of wooden huts on concrete foundations in somewhat sodden ground. As well as several blocks of barracks there was a camp office, guardroom, canteen and chapel.

In May 1946 my father, Rev. Joseph H. Howe, Methodist minister in nearby Oswaldtwistle since 1944, made contact with the camp in Stanhill and applied for permission to visit

5

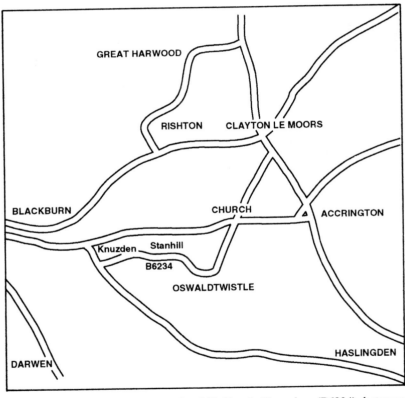

Fig 2: Stanhill Hostel was on Stanhill Road, Knuzden (B6234) between Blackburn and Oswaldtwistle.

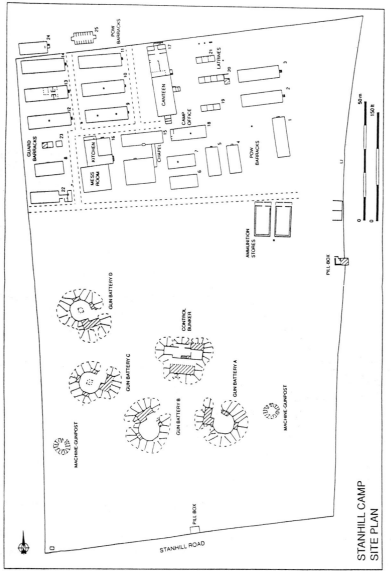

Fig 3: Drawn by Koral Ahmet, The University of Manchester Archeological Unit.

7

the prisoners. On 27 May he was issued with military permit number P19, allowing him 'to enter Stanhill Hostel and nowhere else, for the purpose of Spiritual Ministration' between the hours of 09.00 and 18.00 from 27 May to 26 November 1946, signed on behalf of the Colonel in charge of adminstration in the North West District. Later the permit was extended until 26 May 1947.

In a leaflet of suggestions for the guidance of clergy, the British Council of Churches at that time acknowledged 'hesitation felt by British Clergy on various grounds' which might prevent them from making such contacts. The leaflet pointed out that 'each camp has an interpreter, and a handshake is the same in German as in English'. After many years of thinking of Germans as the enemy, how difficult was it to look on them as fellow human beings? Could clergy and their congregations, who had perhaps lost family members in the war, practise what was preached — love your enemies? It seems my father had no hesitations.

He had been a youth at the time of the First World War. His eighteenth birthday was at the end of August 1918 and he was immediately called up to serve in the forces. However, he applied for exemption from military service on the grounds of his new-found and strongly held Christian belief. His application stated, 'I hold with the teaching of the New Testament as the basis of my belief, that war or the taking of life is murder and therefore contrary to the will of God. There can be no justice in war and force cannot settle disputes, individual, national or international.' This application was not granted but he lodged an appeal against the decision. Either this appeal was successful or the end of the war two months later came in the nick of time. For this short period he undertook agricultural work as a contribution to the war effort. In the Second World War, ministers of religion in Britain were exempt from military service: their ministry to the souls of the people was seen as an essential service to the community.

My father was a kindly, friendly and peace-loving person. Counted among contemporary figures he admired were Mahatma Gandhi, Pastor Martin Niemöller and Dr Donald

8

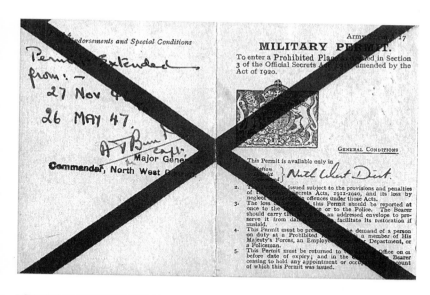

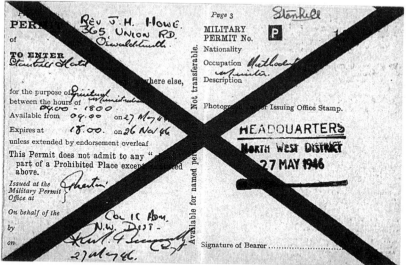

Fig 4: Military permit issued to my father to allow him to enter Stanhill Hostel between certain hours for 'Spiritual Ministration'. Apparently he never signed it!

Soper. Far from having hesitations about contacting the prisoners at Stanhill, he was apparently not satisfied with the limitations of the permit issued to him. He responded as follows:

York House
365 Union Road
Oswaldtwistle
1 June 1946

Dear Sir

Thank you for permit relative to my visits to Stanhill POW Hostel. I shall be pleased to do what I can for the men.

I would point out that the restrictions of permitted hours 9 am to 6 pm precludes any possibility of *evening work*.

At present, while the POWs are not employed outside the camp, the times are all right, but when the men are given work, and therefore not available in the day time, it would appear a useful facility to be able, as occasion requires, to visit the men *after* 6 pm.

Would it be possible, and in order, to *extend* the hours permitted me, so as to make possible evening visitation?

Yours faithfully,
Joseph H. Howe

Later events suggest that this request met with success.

There were more than 200 German prisoners at Stanhill aged between 18 and 46. After camp duties of preparing food, cleaning and keeping fit, the men had some leisure time to fill and energy which could be put to good use. This must have been the situation for the hundreds of thousands of prisoners in the country at that time — healthy men forcibly made idle while there was a great deal of reconstruction work waiting to be done to put the country back on its feet after the war. Housing, for instance, was in crisis. It is estimated that four million houses had been demolished by bombs. Many British soldiers returned from the war to find their families homeless. Some families squatted in ex-army camps. The government's aim was to build a million and a half new homes and so it was decided that prisoners could work under supervision on building sites.

When this idea had first been discussed by Oswaldtwistle's neighbouring town council in Accrington in June 1945, some people had been against it. One alderman said there would be an outburst of feeling in the town. 'When our men came home and saw German prisoners making the streets where they lived they would want to poison them,' he said, referring to servicemen returning from the war. 'The very sight of these Germans would make them ill.' However, those opposed to the idea were assured that prisoners would only be used if no British labour was available and they would be paid at trade-union rates. In other words, they would not be used as cheap labour while English men were being made redundant from declining post-war industry. On 5 June 1945, Accrington Town Council agreed by 23 votes to 3, that prisoners could work on housing sites in the Accrington area. The main concern was to provide sufficient housing for post-war Britain.

Prisoners did indeed start work on housing sites in the area later that year. The *Accrington Observer and Times* reported that two prisoners employed on Fern Gore housing estate escaped at about 3 o'clock on Wednesday afternoon, taking advantage of a heavy mist. Kolf Seidel and Horst Hoferrichter, described as 'Luftwaffe under officers', gave themselves up the following Saturday evening when they were found desperate for food on Darwen moors. They had lived on berries for their three days of freedom.

Even today some people can recall men in dark camp uniforms helping to build houses on the Isle of Man housing estate in Blackburn, to the west of Oswaldtwistle. The trousers had a large P printed above one knee and a large W above the other. There was also a POW patch to be seen on the backs of jackets. Some prisoners were taken from Stanhill to Preston each day to renovate Fulwood Barracks, used for British troops returning from Europe. Other prisoners were involved in repairing roads.

By the time my father received his permit to enter Stanhill Camp, 22,000 prisoners were working on building sites in Britain. A much larger number, approximately 169,000, were employed in agricultural work. Indeed it has been said that one quarter of all the workforce on the land consisted of POW labour. The wage was normally between three and six shillings a week. At this time, prisoners were only allowed out of camps in working parties to undertake these two types of work. At all other times they were confined to the well-guarded camp site.

Conditions at Stanhill, however, were not bad for prisoners. Remembering his time in Stanhill 43 years later, Herr Ernst Pensch of Grosdohren, Germany, recalled that they were treated well and given sufficient food, with those who were working outside the camp receiving slightly more food than the rest. Many prisoners however had been moved about from camp to camp for several years and were longing to go home now that the war was over. Herr Pensch, for example, had been captured on 28 August 1944 in Chalons sur Marne in northern France by American soldiers. He had been taken to a large European camp for six weeks and then shipped to America where he was moved about between camps until March 1946. No contact had been allowed between prisoners and local Americans. He and many other prisoners then travelled by sea to Belgium, believing they would soon be home. They were very disappointed to hear after eight weeks in Belgium that they were to come to England. No-one knew how long they would have to remain here.

Although physical conditions were not bad, many prisoners suffered homesickness and anxiety about their families. Many kinds of mental torment were also experienced. Some wondered why they had been allowed to survive while comrades fighting alongside them had been killed. Others had nightmares of horrific war experiences, waking up in a sweat night after night. Some had lost all hope, hearing bad news from relations and being unable to take any action. In time prisoners learned about actions their own leaders had taken in concentration camps and wondered if they themselves would be labelled as murderers of women and children. Some felt guilt or shame, or lost pride in the homeland for which they had fought so long. The lack of information about when they would be allowed to return home added a demoralising effect.

12

Nevertheless they had survived the war and they knew they would reach home ultimately. The burning question was, when would that be?

Ministers of religion in Germany had not been exempt from military service as had been the case in Britain. Among the German prisoners in Britain there were estimated to be over 150 ordained Protestant ministers. One Protestant and one Roman Catholic military chaplain were allowed per division by German army regulations. However, except for a short period, there were no ordained prisoners at Stanhill. And so it came about that my father became the Protestant padre, and Rev. Father T. Crowley of St Mary's Roman Catholic Church in Oswaldtwistle was appointed the Roman Catholic padre. There was, however, a camp interpreter, Paul Krüger, and he was to find himself translating hymns, initially for use in Stanhill and later for wider use. Here is an example of Herr Krüger's work:

Melodie: 'Cwm Rhondda'

Guide me, O Thou great Jehovah,
Pilgrim through this barren land;
I am weak, but Thou art mighty;
Hold me with Thy powerful hand;
Bread of heaven, Bread of heaven,
Feed me now and evermore.

Open Thou the crystal fountain,
Whence the healing streams shall flow;
Let the fiery, cloudy pillar
Lead me all my journey through;
Strong Deliverer! Strong Deliverer!
Be Thou still my help and shield.

When I tread the verge of Jordan,
Bid my anxious fears subside;
Death of deaths, and hell's destruction,
Land me safe on Canaan's side;
Songs of praises, Songs of praises,
I will ever give to Thee.

Führ' mich, O grosser Jehova,
Pilger durch dies leere Land;
Ich bin schwach, doch Du bist mächtig;
Halte mich mit starker Hand;
Brot des Himmels, Brot des Himmels,
Nähr' mich jetzt und immerdar.

Offne Du die klare Quelle,
Dass der heilsame Strahl fliesst,
Die Feuer — und Wolkensäule
Führe mich auf meinem Weg.
Starker Retter, Starker Retter
Sei stets Hilfe mir und Schutz.

Bin ich dann am Strand des Jordan
Gebiete meinen Angsten Halt,
Tod dem Tode, Tod der Hölle;
Bring nach Kana sicher mich;
Lobeslieder; Lobeslieder
Will ich ewig singen Dir.

13

Fig 5: The chapel in a Nissen hut at Stanhill Hostel, used for both Protestant and Roman Catholic services.

A Nissen hut was fitted out as a chapel and used for both Protestant and Roman Catholic services. Even before my father had a permit to enter the camp he had been making strenuous efforts to obtain Bibles and hymn books in the German language, as his incoming post shows:

The Methodist Church
Royal Navy, Army and Royal Air Force Board
14 May 1946

Dear Mr Howe,
    Your letter to Mr Hornabrook, concerning the Prisoners of War work you are doing, has been passed to me. Actually this work is done for the protestants by the British Council of

14

Churches ... and I have sent your letter on with a note of explanation ...
Rev Joseph Firth

The British Council of Churches
16 May 1946

Dear Mr Howe,

Rev J. Firth has passed on to me your letter ... I wonder if you would just send me the number and address of the Camp.

I am intending to pass your letter on to Cranfield who is heading this up from the chaplaincy side of the war office ...
Rev R.E. Burlingham

The 'Cranfield' referred to was Rev. Charles Cranfield, the British army's chaplain responsible for German pastors and priests in captivity. At this time, we now know, he was systematically visiting many camps. Over 130 camps received one or more visits from him.

The next letter to arrive was from Pastor Birger Forell, a Swede with a special ministry to Germans in camps in Britain:

World's Alliance of the
Young Men's Christian Associations
War Prisoners' Aid
17 May 1946

Dear Sir,

In reply to your inquiry of May 14th I should like to inform you that our organisation regularly supply all German PW camps and hostels in this country with Bibles, New Testaments, hymn books and books of a general kind in German.

I suggest that the camp speaker of the camp in your neighbourhood sends an order to our office at Norton Camp, Mansfield ... signed by him and countersigned by the Acc. Officer as payment may be involved.

We have no hymn books with tunes in stock at present but have recently printed a small hymn book with 50 hymns selected from the official German hymn book. This booklet is obtainable at 1d per copy and can be ordered from our London office on the proper order form. I enclose a copy for your information.

Fiction books are obtainable from the International Red Cross.

Educational books are obtainable from our office at Norton Camp.

The Protestant hymn book printed by our organisation in America is unfortunately not available for PW camps in this country.

Birger Forell

THE METHODIST CHURCH
LONDON NORTH-EAST DISTRICT

ex- Chairman :
Rev. ERNEST BARRETT, M.A.
Tel.: SEVEN KINGS 1430

Secretary of the Synod :
Rev. ALFRED E. BINKS
Tel.: WANSTEAD 3018

562. GREEN LANE,
GOODMAYES,
ILFORD ESSEX

17th May 1946

Dear Mr Howe.

    I have had so many appeals of the kind you make that our German Mission has exhausted all German Bibles and Hymn Books that can be spared; indeed, there are now scarcely sufficient for our own needs.

    However,you might write Rev.A.Goebel, 4 Bourneville Road,London S.E.6, who may know of other sources,perhaps in the Lutheran Church,of obtaining German Bibles but I doubt if he can lay his hands on many German Methodist Hymn Books.Anyhow,try him.You may mention my name. There is only one l in Goebel.

Yours Sincerely,

Ernest Barrett.

Fig 6: Yet another letter unable to help but suggesting a further contact.

British and Foreign Bible Society
15 May 1946
Dear Sir,

In reply to your letter of 13th inst. We have given many thousands of copies of the German new Testament and Psalms to the War Prisoners Aid of the YMCA for distribution in POW Camps, but there seems quite a number of these camps still without copies.

We are sending you 30 copies which we hope you will find helpful.

German Bibles are in short supply. We are sending you three copies which could perhaps be kept for general use.

We do not publish anything apart from the Scriptures, and I am sorry I cannot say where hymns etc in the German language can be obtained. I would however suggest your writing to The War Prisoners Aid of the YMCA ... , also the Society for Promoting Christian Knowledge ...

G. Cowan

My father was aware that the prisoners were also short of ordinary things to help them occupy their leisure time. He felt that games such as chess and dominoes, and books written in German, would help them to pass their time constructively and make living in captivity a little more bearable. One prisoner, Heinz Müller, was teaching English to fellow prisoners, and some other prisoners could read English, so books written in English would also be of help and interest. My father determined to find out whether the people of Oswaldtwistle would be able and willing to contribute some of their possessions for the prisoners' use. How would they respond to a request for such help?

Fig 7: Prisoners outside a camp building. Back row: first left, Heinz Hermann. Front row: first left, Bruno Tietze.

2

Enemies Worship Together

My father was minister of two churches in Oswaldtwistle, Mount Pleasant Methodist Church, which my mother, sister and I attended, and a smaller one, York Street Methodist Church, situated across the street from the manse in which we lived. It was the custom for the minister's family to be members of the larger church despite the manse's proximity to York Street.

On Sunday afternoon, 26 May 1946, my father addressed the Young Men's Class at Mount Pleasant Church. Although his permit was not to come through until later that week, it seems that he had already visited the camp and he described some of the conditions there to the young men present that Sunday afternoon. A Nissen hut served as a chapel but there was no piano or other instrument to accompany hymn singing. The prisoners were short of things to occupy their leisure time. He appealed for any games or books which the young men could spare; he would be glad to take them to the prisoners. Following this meeting, information about the existence of the camp and its inmates now began to spread.

On the very day that the military official was signing my father's permit, a 27-year-old man at Mount Pleasant Methodist Church, Mr Alfred Hindle, a member of the Young Men's Class, was moved to write a letter to the secretary of the Church's Senior Guild, Miss S. Scholes. He hoped that the unusual suggestion he was to make in the letter would be considered at a forthcoming weeknight meeting of the Guild, which, on this occasion, he could not attend in person. He

Fig 8: Mount Pleasant Methodist Church, Oswaldtwistle, much as it was in 1946. Later, it was known as Rhyddings Methodist Church.

wrote as follows:

15 Fielding Lane
Oswaldtwistle
27 May 1946

To: The Secretary
    M.P. Senior Guild
Dear Secretary

On Sunday afternoon the speaker at the Young Men's Class was the Rev J.H. Howe and after his address he made an appeal for games and books on behalf of the German prisoners of war who are imprisoned in the camp up Stanhill.

Now I fully realize that it will be well nigh impossible for him to obtain these games and any suitable books, but after all one of the great beliefs of our Christian Religion is "That mankind is one Great Brotherhood, indivisible alike by social status, religion, nationality or colour, God being the faith of all". I am therefore of the opinion that the nearness of the German p-o-w's and Mr Howe's self imposed task have given the people of Mount Pleasant a chance and a great opportunity that we who have received religious instruction therein must not fail to grasp and that opportunity in my own mind is of showing, not only to the people of our own district but to a few of our German Brothers a little practical Christianity.

I am of the opinion that we could if the authorities are agreeable arrange for any of these p-o-w's who may so wish, to attend the service which is being planned for the afternoon of Sunday, June 30th as part of our Anniversary Celebrations. This service is I believe to be a Service of Praise in a purely musical form with wellknown and popular hymns and probably something special by the Choir, it would therefore I am sure be of interest to the German p-o-w's and there would be no need for an interpreter.

Now I wish you to bring this suggestion forward at the next meeting of the Guild and discuss it from all angles. If it be agreed with, you could bring the suggestion to the notice of the Leaders of the School in order that the necessary arrangements could be made.

I fully realize that there will be arguments for and against this suggestion, but after all we have just gone through six years of war which has undoubtedly bred a great deal of hatred between the peoples of different nations, this hatred is without doubt alien to the teachings of the New Testament in which we who profess to be Christians believe. We who remember the whole of the past six years must and shall be resolved to doing all that we can possibly do to avert any future wars. Wars cannot as some people would have us believe be averted solely by the efforts of world statesmen, but we the common people must assist by helping "To destroy those barriers which separate man from man and substitute for them a Happy Christian Comradeship". This suggestion of mine if adopted can be one step forward in the forming of that comradeship between we of Mount Pleasant and a few Germans involuntarily sojourning in our country.

I know that some people will say let the Germans stew in their own juice, they have brought the world all the miseries of the past six years — have they? It is a debatable point, but even if we grant that they have been solely responsible for all the miseries of the past six years cannot we show some of the mercy and charity of our Christianity as shown in the life and teachings of Jesus.

One reason why I am sending this suggestion to the Guild and not to the Young Men's Class, where I am sure it would be accepted, is because I have recently heard a number of statements to the effect that the youth of today are too much pleasure bent and rather slow at shouldering the responsibilities which are and should be theirs. So I say let the youth of Mount Pleasant give a lead at least in one thing and show that they are not afraid of practising what they preach.

If the suggestion be adopted we could probably follow it up with further services to a mixed congregation at which a short sermon could be given in English and interpreted in German and probably other ministers within the circuit would be only too pleased to assist in these small acts of Christian Charity and thereby relieve Mr Howe of a little of his self imposed extra work. These prisoners have only a Nissen Hut in which to worship and no instrument to lead their hymn singing. Just try to imagine what your own feelings would be in their place if you were to be invited to share the service and chapel and a local Christian body. Remember we of Mount Pleasant have undoubtedly a chapel of which we can be proud and the balcony would I am sure accommodate all who may wish to attend.

I am only sorry that I shall not be able to be at the meeting to present my own case on behalf of these Germans for even though the pen be mightier than the sword, my pen is not I feel sure as mighty as my tongue would be in this instance.

Yours sincerely,

A Hindle

Alfred Hindle and his two older brothers, Fred and Arnold, had all fought in the war between 1940 and 1945. Fred had been a prisoner of war for three years. As Alfred put it, many people would want the Germans to 'stew in their own juice' because they had 'brought the world all the miseries of the last six years'. One would think that the natural feeling after a war in which some of one's friends or relations had been killed or maimed or their homes destroyed would be one of hatred. But the Hindle family had no such feelings. Alfred was able to put himself in the place of the prisoners ('imagine what your own feelings would be ... '). His enthusiasm was catching, and his tact was pertinent ('we of Mount Pleasant have undoubtedly a chapel of which we can be proud'). 1946 was in fact Mount Pleasant's centenary year, the first services having been held in the building on 16 July 1846. At any rate, his suggestions gained support, as the *Accrington Observer and Times* reported in November that year:

> German prisoners of war from Stanhill Camp have been attending the church regularly for some months, and their original inclusion in the services was due in large measure to the representation of the church's returned ex-Servicemen. The Minister (Rev J.H. Howe) was in complete sympathy with the ex-Service members of his congregation and after much effort on his part the services received official sanction.

Over 40 years later, Mr Fred Hindle recalled telling my father that if he felt joint services were right, and if he was doing it for the right reasons, he should 'get it done'.

Official literature at this time stated, however, that although 'The War Office does not object to German POW having services in civilian churches ... the War Office does not allow the German POW to have services *with* the English congregation.' (*Prisoners of War in Great Britain*, British Council of Churches, April 1946.)

Despite this official restriction, before very long prisoners from Stanhill were attending Mount Pleasant Methodist Church once a month for joint Anglo/German services, in addition to services conducted at the camp for the prisoners on their own. Services at Mount Pleasant had to suit both German- and English-speaking worshippers, and a typical order of Sunday morning worship was:

23

Hymn
Prayer in German and then in English
Lord's Prayer in both languages spoken together
Hymn sung by the children
Children's reading and children's address
Hymn sung by German members of the congregation
Bible reading in German and then in English
Announcements and offertory
Hymn
German reading of sermon followed by sermon in English
Hymn
Benediction
Hymn during which Germans retire

All prayers and sermons had therefore to be written out well in advance to allow time for translation. This was carried out initially by one of the prisoners, Heinz Müller, and later, when he left the camp in November 1946, by the camp interpreter, Paul Krüger.

At this time no form of 'fraternisation' was allowed between British worshippers and German prisoners attending services. This explains the need for the extra hymn after the benediction, during which the prisoners rose from their special place, the front pews on the left of the central pulpit, and filed out of the church before the rest of the congregation could leave.

A Register of Attendance at Protestant Services was drawn up by my father, showing the names of 49 prisoners who took part in services between 12 May and 25 August 1946. Heinz Müller marked the register. Services were held either at the camp or at Mount Pleasant Church, weekly or fortnightly. Actual attendance ranged from 15 to 32 per service, and the average was about 24. Later attendance records are incomplete.

My father was acquiring some German vocabulary, as his autumn list of services showed:

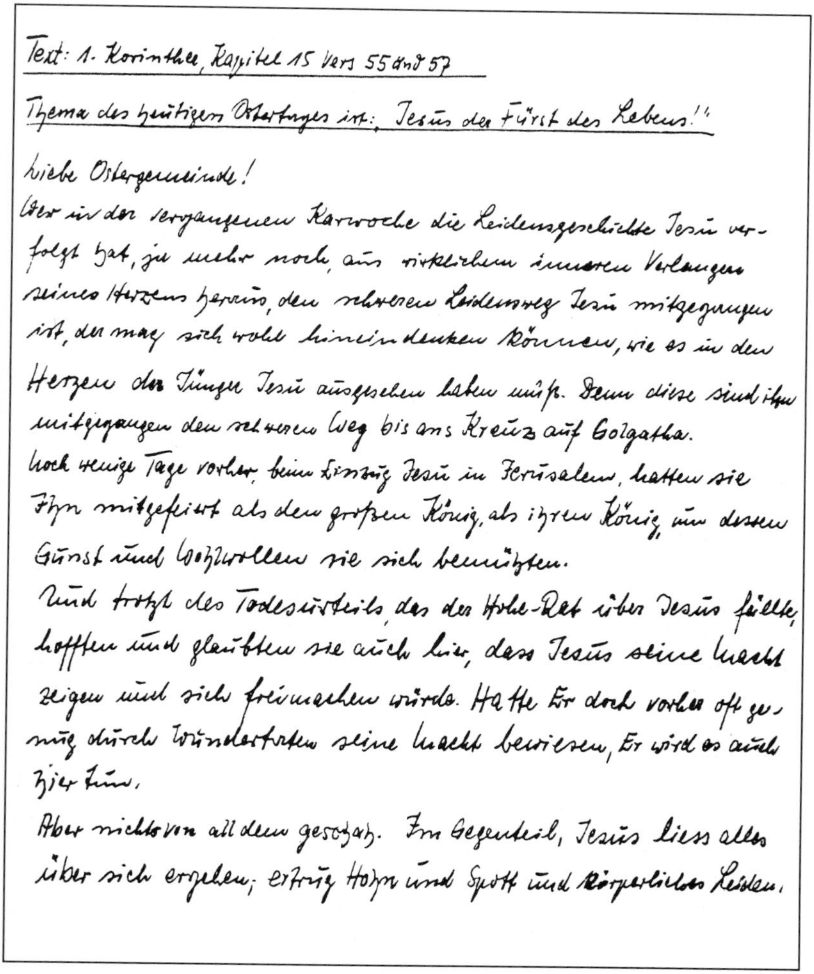

Text: 1. Korinther, Kapitel 15 Vers 55 und 57

Thema des heutigen Ostertages ist: "Jesus der Fürst des Lebens!"

Liebe Ostergemeinde!

Wer in der vergangenen Karwoche die Leidensgeschichte Jesu verfolgt hat, je mehr noch, aus wirklichem inneren Verlangen seines Herzens heraus, den schweren Leidensweg Jesu mitgegangen ist, der mag sich wohl hineindenken können, wie es in den Herzen der Jünger Jesu ausgesehen haben muß. Denn diese sind ihm mitgegangen den schweren Weg bis ans Kreuz auf Golgatha.

Noch wenige Tage vorher, beim Einzug Jesu in Jerusalem, hatten sie Ihn mitgefeiert als den großen König, als ihren König, um dessen Gunst und Wohlwollen sie sich bemühten.

Und trotz des Todesurteils, das der Hohe-Rat über Jesus fällte, hofften und glaubten sie auch hier, dass Jesus seine Macht zeigen und sich freimachen würde. Hatte Er doch vorher oft genug durch Wundertaten seine Macht bewiesen, Er wird es auch hier tun.

Aber nichts von all dem geschah. Im Gegenteil, Jesus ließ alles über sich ergehen; erträgt Hohn und Spott und körperliches Leiden.

Fig 9: Part of a sermon translated into German.

REGISTER OF ATTENDANCE AT SERVICES.
Please mark, and return to Rev. J.W. Howe when
he returns.

Name	July 14	21	28	Aug 4	11	18	25
Heine Muller	/	/	/	/	/	·/	.
Hans Wolf	·/	/	/	/			.
Walter Schwartz	/	/	/	/	/	/	
Emil Schultz	/				/		
Robert Swirkoneski		/	/	/			
Gustav Sonnenberg		/	/	/	L	/	
Karl Khritz							
Marc Welmar							
Wilhelm Schonlau		/	/	/			
Willy Leibeike	/	/	/	/	(	\	
Heinrich v. Winbell	/	/	/	/	/		
Herbert Funk	/	/	/	\			
Kritz Kussatz	/	/	/	/	/		
Rudolf Funtze	/						
Bernard Funtze	/			/	L		
Wilhelm Thom							
Friedrich Weidelieh		/	/	/	c	/	
Georg Maier							
Leonard Luber	/	/	/	\		/	
Guenter Krause	/	/	/	/	(	/	
Richard Schubert	/	/	/	/	(		
Friedrich Zorbach	/	/	/	/	(	(	
Willm Kürzke		/	/	/	(	(	
Jacob Wessner		/		/	(		
Johann Ellerich				/	/		
Georg Rauscher x							
Kurt Schröder ▲							
Ludvig Zwally _	/	/	/	/		/	
Friedk Wittmann				/		/	
Alfred Peters				/	L	:	
Gustav Scheurer		/	/	/	((	(	
Werner Ziemann		/	/	/	(	/	
Ottmar Willuweit.	/	/	/	/	(	(	
Karl Hehring x							
Bruno Schneider				/			
Adolf Rohs ‹							
Fritz Schneider x							
Peter Wollenweber	/						
Johann Lordscheid	/						

Fig 10: This register covered a period when my father was away, possibly at the annual Methodist Conference, followed by a visit to his sister in Northampton and a holiday at St Anne's on Sea.

Der Protestantisch Kirchendeinst
Sept 29 Sonntag. Das Lager. Rev J.H. Howe
Okt 13 Sonntag. 10.30 Mount Pleasant Kirche. J.H. Howe
    27 Sonntag. Das Lager. J.H. Howe
Nov 10 Sonn. Mt Pleasant. 10.30 J.H. Howe
    24 Sonn. Das Lager. J.H. Howe
Dez 8 Sonn. Das Lager. J.H. Howe
    15 Sonn. Mt Pleasant Kirche. Howe
    22 Sonn. Das Lager. Weihnachten Leid. Howe

The complete list also shows Protestant services conducted at the camp on Mondays every fortnight by a P. Schodde, perhaps a visiting German pastor.

Roman Catholic prisoners were by this time attending St Mary's Roman Catholic Church in Oswaldtwistle. A group of prisoners could be seen each Sunday morning marching one and a half miles from the camp to St Mary's. A little later, a second group set off for their two-mile walk from the camp to Mount Pleasant. To people living along the route, Stanhill Road, Stanhill Lane and Union Road, as we at the manse did, this became a familiar Sunday morning sight.

The service held on Sunday 10 November at Mount Pleasant proved to be of particular significance, as it was Remembrance Sunday when those killed in the century's two World Wars were held in mind. The *Accrington Observer and Times* reported it in these words:

German prisoners of war were among the congregation at a service of remembrance held at Mount Pleasant Church, Oswaldtwistle, on Sunday morning.

    There, with heads bowed, they joined their one-time enemies, British ex-Servicemen of two world wars, in silent and reverent homage to the fallen of both sides.

    The choirmaster, Mr F. Hindle, was for over three years a prisoner of war in Germany.

    Service was conducted by the Rev J.H. Howe, and his sermon, which was first read in German by one of the prisoners, was based on the theme of "The New Earth". How great was the need, declared Mr Howe, for men to learn what they ought to have learned long ago — that true power, leadership

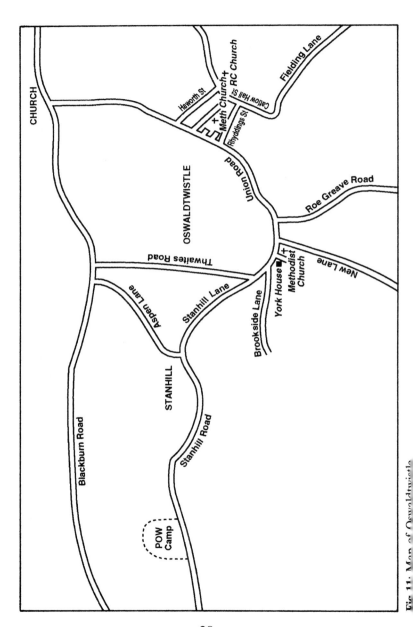

Fig. 11: Map of Oswaldtwistle

among nations as among individuals did not come from mere might or force but was a moral quality. The truth was that they could not build a new world without God. Truth, not one sided propaganda, righteousness, not national or class interest, justice, not vengeance, love and not hatred, nor yet mere tolerance, were the true foundations of a new society ...

Similar joint services were now being held in other parts of the country. Some Germans were surprised to find that the hymn *Glorious Things of Thee are Spoken* was sung in some churches to the tune of their own national anthem, *Deutschland Uber Alles*. The tune was Haydn's *The Emperor's Hymn*. The problem of finding hymns and hymn tunes known to both sections of the congregation, illustrated by previous correspondence, persisted into the following year. My father wrote to a German minister living in England, Rev. Franz Hildebrandt, who replied as follows:

Cambridge Methodist Church
15.1.1947

Dear Mr Howe

... Of the German prisoners I still see quite a bit in my spare time, trying to preach now and then on a Sunday afternoon, and also conducting such joint services as you are holding in your church. The trouble is that no decent translation of the Methodist hymns exist in German; the official German MHB has only about 6 or 7(!) of Wesley's hymns, miserably rendered, among 6–7000 others, and, as you say, the difficulty of meters seem insuperable. I am trying to meet the need by having 2 or 3 hymns sung at the same time in both languages, and 1 or 2 in either English or German only ...

[Here follows a list of hymns which appear in common in English and German hymn books.]

Hymns where the text is the same but the time or metre different, or vice versa, might be sung in turn, first in the one and then in the other language.

It is good to know of the fellowship which has been established between your people and the Prisoners, and I am sure that these services will bear fruit in the future ...

Rev F. Hildebrandt

Sorry this is late

Mr Gibson will send

the 15/- (many thanks Jffh)

LARKE'S TYPEWRITING
& DUPLICATING BUREAU.

PROPRIETOR:- MARY C. CLARKE, M.I.P.S.(T), A.C.T.S., PCT.,

INDIVIDUAL TUITION IN
PITMAN'S SHORTHAND
AND TOUCH - TYPING.

F.I.P.S.(T)

MANUSCRIPTS,
THESES,
LEGAL WORK ETC.,
NEATLY AND
ACCURATELY
EXECUTED.

46A, HENRY STREET, CHURCH. NEAR ACCRINGTON, LANCS.

28th December, 1946.

Rev. J.. H. Howe,
York House,
OSWALDTWISTLE.

To duplicating:- 200 Hymn Sheet for German Prisoners ... 6/0d

Received with thanks
18th January, 1947,

M. C. Clarke

Fig 12: Bill for the duplicating of hymn sheets.

On the same subject of hymns known to both Germans and English, a further letter arrived.

25 City Road, London
14 January 1947

Dear Mr Howe,
You will have heard from Mr Barton about the suggestion of printing hymns for the POWs. I was very interested in the sug-

gestion and took it up with Dr Kramm. He sent me a book which I enclose ... I had already suggested the hymn sheets to him, and you will see his note of suggested hymns. I hope this will be of some help to you ...

Rev Leslie F. Church

Before this time, however, my father had taken it into his own hands to produce hymn sheets to fit the local situation. Miss Mary C. Clarke of Clarke's Typewriting and Duplicating Bureau typed a hymn sheet and duplicated 200 copies at a cost of '6 shillings to you!' — and this was one of many.

Where a tune was known by both German and English worshippers, it could be sung simultaneously in both languages. As it happened, the German tune *Lobe den Herren* was in the British Methodist Hymn Book set to the hymn *Praise to the Lord* but was not known to the English congregation at Mount Pleasant at that time. My father asked the choirmaster, Mr Fred Hindle, to teach the choir and the congregation this tune, and it thus became part of the repertoire for joint services.

As Christmas 1946 approached, Mount Pleasant Sunday School decided to raise money to pay for a Christmas card to be sent to each prisoner, and the duplicating for this innovative venture was entrusted to the same Miss Mary Clarke.

GLÜCKLICH
WEIHNACHTEN
1 9 4 6 .

Mit herzlichen Christliche Grüssen
zu Weihnachtstag

von

Mount Pleasant Methodist Kirche,
Oswaldtwistle, England,

Von Pastor, Gemeinde und die
Sonntagschule Kinder.

Joseph H. Howe

Fig 13: Duplicated Christmas card sent to prisoners at Stanhill and paid for by Mount Pleasant Sunday School.

3

Christmas 1946

Christmas cards written in German and sent to every prisoner was but one of the ideas planned for Christmas 1946. Arrangements were made for Accrington Male Voice Choir to visit the camp on the Sunday before Christmas to give a concert. This choir, still in existence, had been founded by Mr Milton Holgate shortly after the end of the First World War in 1919, and he was still the conductor at the time of the visit to the camp.

The most radical idea planned, however, was that some prisoners were to be allowed to spend Christmas Day in the homes of members of the Methodist and Roman Catholic congregations in Oswaldtwistle. Which households would welcome such a visitor? Some of those eager to show friendship and offer hospitality to the prisoners had themselves been prisoners of war in Germany, Italy or Japan.

But first came the visit of the fifty-strong Male Voice Choir. It was a momentous occasion for the choir itself and for more than 200 prisoners who gathered in the camp canteen, as the newspaper reports show. The *Accrington Observer and Times* for the following Tuesday (price one penny) printed the report as its first article on page one:

Through driving rain, along unlighted roads on a moonless night that brought back memories of some of the more unpleasant experiences of the black-out, and stumbling in and out of pools of water between rows of wooden huts, the singers arrived by car and on foot, some making their way across

33

country from their homes at Rishton.

The bare walls of the canteen, normally relieved only by the official camp notices, were decorated with fir boughs and ferns, lightly besprinkled with tufts of cotton wool, giving the appearance of snow flakes ...

Probably never before has the choir had so appreciative an audience. From the first to the last note of each number they sat in absolute silence. Enraptured by the flow of melody from the massed singers, their gaze never wavered from the faces of the men on the dais.

Opening the concert with two verses from the hymn "Jesus Shall Reign", to the tune of "Accrington", Mr Milton Holgate conducted the choir through the "Jolly Roger" and the "Fishermen of England", the solo in which was taken by Mr F. Chadwick. Then, apparently feeling the combined effect of the heat in the building and his own exertions, Mr Holgate removed his jacket and waistcoat amid roars of friendly laughter from the audience, who thoroughly enjoyed this homely gesture.

The choir's rendering of two German folk songs aroused nostalgic memories among the prisoners. Eyes gazed into space as, for them, walls faded and they were for a brief moment mentally reunited with their families. The spell was broken gradually as Mr Holgate turned and motioned to the prisoners to join in the singing of "Two Roses". Slowly their voices built up to a determined crescendo, and, singing lustily, they followed the conductor's compelling hands with hardly a fault. Imperceptibly, the choir sang more quietly until at the end they were silent, and the voices of the men they had journeyed to entertain could be heard.

Then came the turn of the prisoners, each of whom had been given a sheet on which were printed in German three well known Christmas hymns. There was no note of incongruity when, singing in English, the choir was joined by 200 odd German voices in "Oh, Come all ye Faithful". There was a depth of feeling in the full throated tones which overcame all language barriers as the voices resounded to almost roof-shaking volume.

Following a short interval, during which the prisoners were permitted to smoke, the second half opened with the rousing "Soldiers Chorus" from Gounod's "Faust". Mr J. Smith's solo

34

in "Moira, My Girl", was loudly applauded, as was also the full choir's rendering of "Comrades in Arms".

After the prisoners themselves had sung "Good Christian Men, Rejoice" and "Stille Nacht" in their native tongue, the choir sang "Silent Night".

"I think the whole choir enjoyed the experience", stated Mr Holgate. "I certainly did and we found them to be a very appreciative audience — and they have some quite good singers among them as well. There were members of my own family in the forces during the war, and I'd like to think that if any of them had been taken prisoner someone in Germany would have done something on similar lines. The choir responded in grand style to the invitation to sing here. Perhaps in our own way we may be doing something that will help to prevent any recurrence of the events of the past six years."

But the prisoners themselves also had a surprise for the people of Oswaldtwistle. Despite having no tools except pen-knives, they had for some time been making wooden toys for the Sunday School children. Under the heading 'POWs Say "Thank You" With Toys', the *Northern Daily Telegraph*, printed in Blackburn, carried the following story on Christmas Eve:

Toys carved out of wood with pen knives have been presented by German POWs at Stanhill Camp, Oswaldtwistle, to children of Mount Pleasant Methodist and St Mary's Roman Catholic Sunday Schools. This is their "Thank you" for work the minister and priest and congregations have done on their behalf.

Much ingenuity has been shown by the POWs in making the toys, which include a dolls house with furniture, doll's pram, motor-lorry, plane, wheel-barrow, rocking horse, and dogs with wagging tails.

Another newspaper account mentions ducks with wings which flapped when drawn along the ground, a dancing clown, and slippers woven from lengths of rope and string. Made from odd pieces of wood and patiently carved with penknives, the toys were painted in contrasting colours. 'They

Fig 14: German POWs with the toys they made for children in Oswald-twistle, Christmas 1946. Also in the picture, some members of Accrington Male Voice Choir.

have been very good to us,' one English-speaking prisoner said about the people of Oswaldtwistle. 'It is a thank offering from us to the children, and though it is not much, for we have no tools, we are grateful and happy to make them.' (*Accrington Observer and Times*, 24 December 1946.)

My father kept a diary of his thoughts over the Christmas period. The entry for Sunday 22 December shows that the making of the toys had been kept a secret even from him. He writes:

> In the canteen, arrayed on either side of the platform, were tables filled with toys. To my surprise, I was told that the Germans have made these toys for the children of Mount Pleasant Sunday School and St Mary's Roman Catholic Church. It is a touching expression of the gratitude of the men for what little we have done for them.

His diary continues:

Monday 23rd. An appeal from the Camp for more Christmas tree decorations sent me into town today. I found very little suitable material available. In one shop there was a supply of tinsel. When the proprietor heard I was purchasing this for the Camp, he offered me the lot for a few shillings. Before I could pay for it a lady in the shop stepped forward and said "I will pay for that; there is so little we can do for these men."

Newspaper publicity in the week before Christmas had repercussions. A lady from Lower Darwen twice visited the manse to bring books written in German. Among them was a large-print German Bible which was placed on the altar in the camp chapel. This Bible, with the inscription 'Ex Libris A H Wilson', is still in my possession.

The 'German helper', referred to in my father's diary for Christmas Eve, as follows, was a prisoner called Walter Schwarz. My father's first helper, Heinz Müller, had been fortunate enough to be sent back home to Germany in November. This was a loss to my father, as Heinz was a mature person, fluent in English, with whom my father had formed a real friendship. Walter was a younger man with only a little English, but a very willing helper. The diary reads:

Tuesday 24th. My Circuit duties did not permit me to take the special Christmas Eve service for the prisoners in the Camp Chapel, but my German helper conducted the service which I had prepared. Later the Roman Catholics had midnight Mass in the same Chapel.

I was able to pay a friendly call in the evening to see the Christmas Tree, the gift of Quaker sympathisers. And what a tree! So shiningly decorated, tinsel, "angel hair", and little cakes. The men were just dispersing after their Christmas Eve party, and making their way to their barracks where they continued their celebrations in smaller "house" groups. I was asked by my helper to see his barracks, and found myself among 17 Germans who were prepared to entertain me. This was a pleasant surprise. After a welcome I took refreshment with them and tried out a few German phrases.

We found it not difficult to understand each other, for several spoke English, and in any case the spirit of fellowship needs no interpreter. Here again was a large Christmas tree, decorated and illuminated.

Word came that I was invited to attend yet another little gathering "in half an hour". So, after a visit to the British Office, where I was able to arrange for further Christmas day hospitality, I made my way to the "Barber's Shop", now transformed into a cosy room, and prepared for a simple meal. The meal we ate in candle-light. Here were gathered the Camp Interpreter, Camp Leader, hairdresser, clerk, policeman, and other important people. I referred to the gathering as the "House of Lords" a joke not lost on the company. English was freely spoken and we talked of many things ... of those classic films of pre-war days which Germany could produce so well; of the desire of our people for peace and understanding; of the usefulness of inter-visitation among young people of both our countries. The time passed all too quickly: the candles on the tree burned low.

There was time on my homeward walk along the moorland road, to reflect on these things. Will this enforced sojourn in our land give these men an insight into our deep desire to live in peace with their nation, so great in days past? Perhaps Christmas 1946 will help, for tomorrow is Christmas Day, and invitations have come daily from those who wish to entertain the Germans.

Among the unusual scenes reported in the camp that evening was that of British guards shaking hands with their prisoners, exchanging Christmas greetings, and showing each other photographs of their wives and sweethearts.

The idea of entertaining a German prisoner in your home for Christmas Day caught on in the lead-up to Christmas. At first it was said that about a dozen men would make these visits. Further arrangements were made after the choir's visit to the camp, and in the event over 60 of the 200 or so men at the camp were catered for. Some more good news was to be heard before the end of Christmas Day itself. My father's diary continues:

Christmas Day. This morning over sixty of the prisoners attended my service at Mount Pleasant Church. A similar number would attend the Roman Catholic Church nearby. For the first time the men walked to church in little groups instead of marching down in formation. The service was of real spiritual power. We sang together carols in both languages. "Christians Awake" was sung in English, and the Germans sang by themselves their carol "O Du Froliche". Their voices resounded in the church. The words were unfamiliar, but the tune "Sicilian Mariners" was of course well known to us, and conveyed the joyousness of the carol. The familiar account from Luke of the birth of Jesus was read, and instead of a sermon, a message from a German Pastor to the people of Germany given a few years ago, but still pertinent, was read, first in German and then in English. After the service, the congregation "fraternised" for the first time. Christmas greetings were exchanged readily in both languages.

Then came the unique privilege of introducing for the first time German prisoners and English hosts who were to spend the rest of the day in each other's company. A number of the hosts were ex-servicemen and three had themselves been prisoners of war, one in Japanese hands, and the others in Italy and Germany.

The joy of effecting these introductions was exceeded only by the sense of pleasure as at nine o'clock in the evening, I saw the men accompanied by their hosts, returning to the Camp. On every hand was the sense of gratitude and delight. Friendships have been formed that will last through the years. Stories have come in of happy parties. If any feared that the presence of a German would prove an hindrance to their own pleasure, that fear has been dispelled. Where there were children, the men quickly found themselves "at home" with the young people. If pleasure has been given to the German guests, the families entertaining them have not gone unrewarded.

The *Accrington Observer and Times* was again on the scene to report the barely believable events, under the headline

'German Prisoners of War were guests in local homes' (28 December 1946):

Enmities fostered by six years of bitter warfare are forgotten in the "peace on Earth. Goodwill to all men" spirit of Yuletide when German prisoners of war joined British ex-Servicemen and their families at the festive board on Christmas Day. Over 30 families in the Oswaldtwistle, Knuzden and Accrington area took advantage of the recent relaxation of Home Office regulations to invite German prisoners of War from the camp at Stanhill, and 60 delighted prisoners found themselves, for the first time since they marched with the Fuehrer's Legions, enjoying all the festivities of a traditional domestic Christmas.

They tucked into the seasonable fare with a will, joined in the family games, and in many households proved themselves prime favourites with the youngsters, with whom they romped on the carpets and joined wholeheartedly in their makebelieve.

The language difficulties seem to have been small deterrent to the carnival atmosphere, and in several of the homes in which they were guests at least one person spoke either German or alternatively English.

At nine pm when the POWs had to return, the great majority of them were laughing and joking with their hosts, and at the gates of the camp "Good nights" and good wishes were expressed in two languages ...

Among the invitations were requests for 6, 4 or 3 prisoners. A few were invited out to tea only, but by far the greater number received invitations for the full period — from 9 in the morning until 9 at night ... Mr Howe said "I think the invitations have resulted in a far greater degree of fellowship. I know of no case where this extra freedom has been abused in any way."

Mr Fred Hindle, the choirmaster, was one of those whose family entertained a prisoner. Over 40 years later he was able to recall going into the minister's vestry that Christmas morning to be allocated a prisoner, and signing an undertaking to return him to the camp in the evening. As a prisoner of war in Italy and Czechoslovakia from 1942 to 1945, Mr

Hindle had known what it was like to exist on a roll of black bread and a bowl of skilly each day. (Skilly was a thin soup containing dandelions, grass or anything else just edible.) Mr Hindle weighed 15 stones 2 pounds when captured and 7 stones 10 pounds when he returned home on his birthday, 29 June 1945. Despite these recent experiences, the family of Mr Fred Hindle senior did not hesitate to offer hospitality to a German prisoner.

My father's diary continues with reflections on the day's events:

> Can we measure the effect of this happening? This is the first time for three, four, five or even, in some cases, six years that the Germans have entered a private home. Our only regret has been that we could not entertain all the men from the camp. Over sixty out of more than two hundred were provided for.
>
> In the manse the first reminder of our German friends came early in the morning, in the form of a gift — per Saint Nicholas — of a doll's house, complete with furniture to scale. It was the work of the prisoners, and sent for the minister's children. Each article is perfect, and reflects the skill and patience of the men who have made this, and all the toys presented, without proper tools for the purpose.
>
> Our own guest was the friend who has helped me so much in the conduct of worship lately; one of the group of men who have never missed the Protestant Services, either in Camp or in Church. It was delightful to have him and to see him taking part in the games in our home. How quickly he learnt the games which were new to him! We saw his photographs of home, kindred, and of the girl who waits for his return.

I first saw the wooden dolls' house made by the prisoners on Christmas morning 1946 in the dining room at the front of our house. At the age of seven I was told that all presents came from Father Christmas but somehow I always knew that the dolls' house was made by German prisoners. It appeared like a stage setting of two rooms next to each other (see centre front of picture on page 36) without a front, an upstairs or a roof. At the age of twelve my sister was perhaps

Fig 15: The Manse, 'York House', 365 Union Road, Oswaldtwistle. Photograph taken in 1989. This was our house from 1944 to 1949. Part of York Street Methodist Church can be seen on the left of the picture.

too old for it, and the dolls' house seemed to belong to me. It was a magnificent present.

Not surprisingly, the German prisoner who was chosen to spend Christmas Day at our house was Walter Schwarz who had taken over as my father's chief helper after Heinz Müller's repatriation.

In those days our Christmas celebrations were large family affairs. My mother's married sister and brother and their respective spouses and children all came to stay from a distance, bringing their food coupons with them. (It was impossible to obtain basic foodstuffs without coupons.) The senior person present was my maternal grandmother. When my 16-year-old cousin heard that a German soldier would be with us on Christmas Day, he could not believe his ears. The past six years had impressed upon children as well as adults that the Germans were the hated and dreaded enemies wanting nothing better than to kill us all. How could we share our annual happy Christmas parties with an enemy? My father's innocent comment that Herr Schwarz's name, translated into English, was Mr Black, did nothing to alleviate the apprehension!

However, when he arrived, Walter's politeness and friendliness soon swept all doubts aside, and my grandmother was most impressed by his courteousness. I was only seven years old at the time, my sister was twelve. Her recollection of Walter is of a short, dark, pale-faced man, gentle and quietly kind. Although he could speak very little English he communicated a natural personal interest in us, especially in our grandmother as matriarch of the family.

There was to be further good news, as my father recorded in his diary:

Welcome news came through in the closing hours of the day. More restrictions are to be relaxed. The men will be allowed to walk freely within a radius of five miles of the Camp: they will be allowed to speak to the people they meet: they will be able to enter the homes of our people at the discretion of the Camp Commandant. Invitations are already to hand. More personal contacts will be made and the work of healing the wounds of war will be extended.

It seems that my father and other people in Oswaldtwistle heard about these relaxations on Christmas Day. The announcement had in fact been made by the government on 12 December, and without it the Christmas Day visits would not have been permitted. The extra details which now became common knowledge meant that prisoners were allowed to stay out till 10 p.m., accept small gifts such as sweets and tobacco, play football against British teams, and ride in private cars (although not many ordinary people had cars in those days). Thus the men could be out walking during the evenings from the time they finished their daily camp duties. They were not, however, allowed to 'enter any place of public entertainment, club or hostel, even by invitation'. This included public houses, restaurants, and cinemas. Nor were they allowed to travel on public transport or make amorous relationships.

The final part of my father's Christmas diary reads as follows:

Thursday 26th. How the men rejoice in this freedom! Rain or no rain, there has been a constant passing on the road before the manse, little groups of Germans who may now come into the more populous parts of the township. "Hello" and "Good Morning" are exchanged freely.

We had our own Boxing Day party at Mount Pleasant, so that I could not meet the German Methodist Pastor who visited the camp today. But the Germans have been in our minds, for we have distributed the toys which they made. We supplied each child present between the ages of five and eight. What delight the toys have given to the recipients!

The local newspapers have been generous in their space for the reports of our Camp activities. They have sent their cameramen, and have covered the stories well. Their publicity has widened the interest in our doings. The Camp Commandant and his staff have from the beginning been most helpful.

The diary "Weihnachten 1946" ends, but the story of human contacts, and kindly Christian hospitality, live on in the hearts of German men. We who have shared the experience of these days are better for it all, and richer in spiritual blessing.
Joseph H. Howe

A few days later a letter arrived for my Father:

Dear Sir,
On behalf of the Protestant congregation of hostel Stanhill I want to express our warmest thanks to you and all members of your congregation. It was for us, having been in captivity for years yet, a Christmas we will never forget.

Thereby you have given us inexpressible joy and we don't know how to thank you for that. We can only ask God He might bless your work, and that therefrom might develop a true love amongst all nations so we will become one community, the community of Christ.

We wish you and your congregation a happy and healthy to God commended New Year!

Yours sincerely,
Walter Schwarz

Home-made Christmas cards had also been sent from the camp. Time would show that Christmas 1946 was indeed something that stayed in the minds and memories of very many of those involved, both German and English, for many years to come. It was full of happy and emotional memories.

Before Christmas, when my father had visited Miss Mary Clarke at her Typewriting and Duplicating Bureau to arrange the printing of the hymn leaflets and Christmas cards, he had told her of the impending arrangements for Christmas Day in Oswaldtwistle. Mary herself attended Antley Methodist Church in Accrington, as she lived in the village of Church near Accrington. However, she showed an interest in the planned events as she spoke some German. She was also musical, singing solos and duets and playing the piano and cello. It was therefore arranged that she should come to the Christmas morning service at Mount Pleasant and sing *Stille Nacht* in German. Mary lived with her father at the grocer's shop in Maden Street, Church. She told my father that if there were any prisoners without an invitation to dinner on Christmas Day she was sure that her father would not mind her offering hospitality. So it came about that Mary took Ernst Pensch home from the service for lunch and tea. She remembers to this day how they sang songs around the piano: Ernst had tears in his eyes as they sang.

On Boxing Day Ernst appeared at the house door, round the corner from the shop, with two friends from the camp, Willi Lubecke and one whose name is now forgotten. Willi's father had been a prisoner of war in the First World War and had made friends with some English people then.

Forty-three years later Herr Pensch recalled his visit to the home of Mr Clarke and his daughter Mary. He too remembered that Mary had played the piano and they had sung *Still*

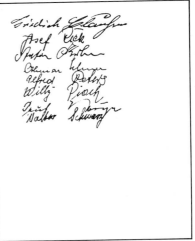

Fig 16: Home-made Christmas cards, signed by some of the prisoners.

the Night in both languages. It had been an extremely moving occasion for him.

Another prisoner, Heinz Hermann was given hospitality on Christmas Day by Mr and Mrs Bill Rawcliffe and their daughter Sheila. In 1990 Herr Hermann described that day in a letter to me:

It began at Christmas-Morning 1946 in the Church Mountpleasant. For myself it was the third Christmas in captivity. My pals and myself we were listening the Christmas-Service. I still remember that during the service a Lady was singing the Christmas-Song "Holy Night, silent Night" in German language. For us all it was very emotional. And after the service and from this day on, all German Prisoners were allowed through the English Government, to get in contact with English People. So after Church we could shake hands with the Church-People and they wished us all a Merry Christmas. And as your father had before requested to every family, to take one German Prisoner to their home for a Christmas-Meal. We were very delighted to come after such a long time in a private house and to have a Christmas-Meal.

Mr Fred Haworth and his wife Kathleen were a young couple with a one-year-old baby at this time. My father had married them at York Street Church in February 1945, so, although they were now living in Accrington, they kept in touch with York Street, which Kathleen had attended before her marriage. They therefore came to hear of my father's appeal for hospitality in private homes for prisoners on Christmas Day. As Mr Haworth recalled decades later, 'On Christmas Day there arrived on our doorstep two men Franz Winschuh and Fritz Herold, neither man able to speak any English and we no German. Nevertheless we established a contact which grew into a friendship.'

Some people still recall minor happenings from that far-off Christmas day. Mr Bert Duxbury remembers the dish of pickled onions on the dinner table. When the meal was over they were surprised to see their German guest take and eat an onion. Not being sure whether he thought it was a sweet, or

47

Fig 17: Heinz Hermann aged 23, photographed in the garden of his new English friends, Mr and Mrs Bill Rawcliffe.

whether that was what Germans did, no-one said anything!

The success of Christmas 1946 led to further contacts between prisoners and local people. At the request of the prisoners a special service was held at York Street Methodist Church on New Year's Day. The Society of Friends (Quakers) loaned a piano to the camp and a group from Blackburn visited the camp on 6 January 1947. A list in pencil shows seven families due to have one or two prisoners to dinner or tea on a Sunday in January. Church members provided flowers for the camp chapel's altar.

Some families who had entertained prisoners on Christmas Day decided to keep up the contact. Heinz Hermann writes:

Since this day nearly every pal of us had contact and friendship to a family of the Church-People in Oswaldtwistle. My pals and myself we were invited for nearly every Sunday for dinner. I myself and three other pals of us we went every Sunday together with our friends Mr and Mrs B. Rawcliffe to Church at Yorkstreet-Chapel and then after the service we were invited for dinner and tea. And then we had to be back at the Camp by darkness. This all made us the life as german prisoners easier and I must say, we all were very happy during this time.

While Heinz was spending Christmas afternoon with Mr and Mrs Rawcliffe, their relatives were also giving hospitality to other prisoners. As was the custom, all these family members came together for Christmas Day tea. Thus it came about that six prisoners were included in the large tea party at Mr and Mrs Rawcliffe's house on Christmas Day. Many friendships developed from this occasion. Bruno Tietze, for example, became friendly with Mr Joe Aspinall's family and helped on his poultry farm when he had time.

Mr and Mrs Fred Haworth often invited their prisoners, Franz Winschuh and Fritz Herold, for Sunday tea whenever their duties at the camp would permit. Mr Haworth writes:

In time another POW came to us, Werner Jungnichkel, an older man who prior to joining the army kept a hotel at Erzgebirge near Dresden, a family man with a wife and two daugh-

49

Fig 18: Bruno Tietze helping on the poultry farm owned by Councillor Joe Aspinall in May 1947. The boys are Joe's son Alfred aged 13 and his cousin Bill Rawcliffe aged 9. The letters P and W (for Prisoner of War) can be seen on Bruno's trousers.

ters back home. He was most appreciative of the chance to share something of our family life, particularly making a great fuss of our baby daughter Anne. One advantage in having Werner with us was that he could speak tolerable English and so was able to include the other two in our conversations so that our friendship was enriched.

Mr Haworth's letter throws further light on the life of the prisoners:

We went out for walks together and introduced them to family and friends alike and in the main they were well received ... Franz was a keen footballer and so on occasions we watched Blackburn Rovers, and because POWs were not at that time allowed on public transport we had to walk it there and back but it was still worth it for the obvious pleasure it gave.

Fig 20: Werner Jungnichkel and Fritz Herold.

Fig 19: Fritz Herold wearing his naval trousers with wide bottoms.

51

Fig 21: Werner, Fritz, Fred Haworth, Fred's sister holding baby Anne, Phyllis Bailey (Fred's sister-in-law), and Fred's wife, Kathleen. Taken outside Fred's mother's house, 73 Fountain Street, Accrington.

All three men worked in the cookhouse at Stanhill and were not always off duty together. Werner was the true cook and confectioner and as my wife was a baker and confectioner they had much in common. He could turn out some very nice stuff, in our kitchen with wartime rations at that time.

The walk from Mr and Mrs Haworth's house in Accrington to Blackburn Rovers football ground was a good five miles in each direction. Fritz had been in the navy and often wore his navy-blue trousers with wide bottoms. Franz had been in captivity some years having spent part of that time in the USA where he recalled with dislike the cotton-picking he and his fellow prisoners had been forced to do. It was perhaps only fair that, of the three, Franz was to be the first to be repatriated.

Repeat Performance

Male Voice Choir Entertain German P.O.W.s

Under the conductorship of Mr. Milton Holgate, Accrington Male Voice Choir gave their second concert at Stanhill P.O.W. camp on Wednesday evening. The programme was a varied one and was enthusiastically received by the large company.

The words of the part songs were translated in advance by Mr. Weber, of Oswaldtwistle, and read by Herr Paul Kruger, the camp interpreter, before the songs were sung. Mr. Milton Holgate's racy comments as the programme proceeded were also translated by Herr Kruger, and certainly appealed to the men's sense of humour.

Several pieces popular with English audiences proved equally acceptable to the Germans. The "Comrades Song of Hope" and the "Soldiers Chorus" from "Faust" being particularly enjoyed. Five Salvationists from the Burnley Citadel Band—the four brothers Clulow and Mr. Fenwick—contributed brass quartettes, quintettes and solos. Mr. F. Chadwick, a member of the choir, gave solos, and Mr. J. Greenwood was the accompanist.

Several hymns of German origin were sung in both languages by the whole company, and "Cwm Rhondda" was introduced to the Germans who sang the translated version very effectively.

Coun. W. W. Cocker, O.B.E., M.A., president of the choir, addressed the men. He and Mr. Holgate expressed the hope that Britain and Germany might live in lasting friendship. Herr Kruger and the Rev. Joseph H. Howe (Protestant padre) expressed thanks to the choir, brass quintette and accompanist for their generous help.

Fig 22: From the *Accrington Observer and Times*, 22 February 1947.

Music, an international currency, acted many times as a bridge between local people and the prisoners. A letter dated 14 January 1947 concerns plans for prisoners to be invited to attend a concert by Burnley Municipal College Orchestra. A Gramophone Concert with duplicated programme in German was given at the camp on 13 February, arranged by Mr Harold Barnes. Mr Barnes was a member of York Street Methodist Church, and a local preacher, who was known to have a good collection of records.

Less than two months elapsed before a further visit to the camp was arranged by Accrington Male Voice Choir which had been such a success on 24 December. Again the *Accring-*

ton Observer and Times told the story, in its issue of 22 February 1947.

People who didn't visit the camp personally found other ways to help. From Blackburn Men's Bible Class Association came more than one cheque:

Cherry Tree
Blackburn
21.1.47

Dear Mr Howe
    I am glad to be able to enclose further cheque to help you in your work with POW Stanhill ...

and later in the year:

> ... We were very proud and thankful to have been able to assist you in a small way in this matter and most sincerely hope that lasting good may be the outcome in many a heart and home.
>   With thanks and warmest greetings,
>
> Arnold Ashworth

But what of people who were not so well-disposed towards those whom they still regarded as the enemy? Some ill-feeling was indeed experienced. There were neighbours who wouldn't speak to those who were showing friendship to the prisoners. All mellowed with time and some admitted later how wrong they had been. When asked why she was making friends with Germans, one person replied, 'If my son was out there I would only wish there was a family to look after him.' One prisoner, who became friendly with a local girl and later married her, recalled only the 'odd bit of friction'. His experience was that British men who had fought in the war could understand both sides and did not cause any trouble.

Let it not be thought that Oswaldtwistle was unique in creating warm relationships between local people and prisoners of war. In Northampton, a Baptist minister arranged a chess match in his church rooms on a Saturday afternoon.

A STUDY in concentration as the Rev. G. C. Beach (on left) county chess champion. plays simultaneous games with German prisoners-of-war at Kingsthorpe Baptist rooms, Northampton. Mr. Beach played 11 games. (Story on Page Three)

Fig 23: From a Northamptonshire newspaper.

Rev. G.C. Beach, vicar of Moulton, and county chess champion, played eleven German prisoners simultaneously. (Mr Beach won seven matches, drew five and lost three.) Most of the games were said to be well-contested and play lasted nearly four hours.

Fifty years later, Miss Kath Humphreys of London remembers how German prisoners came from a camp on Shooters Hill near Woolwich to attend services at Welling Methodist Church and also joined in a midweek club at the Church.

Someone else recalls how his mother, a nurse, made friends with a German Baptist pastor who was admitted to the hospital where she worked. She managed to arrange for him to visit her family home and attend the local church.

In Market Harborough, a watercolour painting of the Methodist Church was presented to the minister by two German prisoners 'in appreciation of the kindness' shown to them.

German Prisoners' Gift to Methodists

A water-colour painting of the Market Harborough Methodist Church being presented to the minister, the Rev. H. G. Lowe, by two German prisoners of war "in appreciation of the kindness shown to the prisoners." Also in the picture are Mr. F. E. Burbridge and Mr. S. Whicher, the circuit stewards.

Fig 24: From the *Methodist Recorder*, 12 December 1946.

A rather special camp had been opened in June 1945 in Norton near Mansfield in Nottinghamshire. It was the brainchild of Pastor Birger Forell of the YMCA and was supported by the War Office. German prisoners who were theological students or teachers in training were sent to Norton to continue their studies. The camp also provided refresher courses for pastors and training for youth leaders. One musically gifted prisoner at Norton organised a choir and drew large congregations to the local church in Cuckney by his amazing organ playing. A puppet theatre at the camp entertained local people.

Relationships in the locality of Norton camp were such that 29 of the former prisoners held a reunion at the site 50 years later, in 1995. One 97-year-old lady in a wheelchair turned out to greet them, having provided hospitality for 'some mother's son' in need of a cup of tea (the first of many) 50 years before. Another person brought with her a wooden toy she had been given by a prisoner for Christmas. One former prisoner was reunited with a lady carrying an autograph album in which he had drawn a picture of her brother. One German recalled after half a century how a family who had befriended him also trusted him. When they were to be out one Sunday afternoon, the usual visiting day, they left the house key under a stone in the garden, so he could let himself in to make a cup of tea and warm himself by the fire until the family returned.

The Roman Catholic commandant of Norton camp, Major A.E. Boughton, gave the camp a motto, *Fide non armis* (Through faith not weapons). He was so dedicated to his German prisoners that he was asked if he was pro-German, perhaps a term of abuse at this point in history. 'No,' he replied, 'I am pro-humanity.'

By February 1947 a few of the prisoners at Stanhill were being sent home. Some were moved to other camps in preparation for the closure of Stanhill camp later in the year. Heinz Hermann was one of those who was happy not to be moved to another camp immediately so he could continue his friendship with Mr and Mrs Rawcliffe and family. (On one occasion they borrowed a suit so that Heinz could accompany the family to a cinema, where prisoners were not permitted to go.) Heinz had in fact been moved about many times since his capture on D Day, 6 June 1944, on the Normandy beaches. He was one of those prisoners at the camp who had spent nearly two years in Florida, seven weeks in Belgium, and shorter stays in two or three other camps in Lancashire. In the summer of 1947 Stanhill camp was closed and Heinz experienced half a dozen other camps in the north of England before being sent home. He wrote to me in 1990, recalling his experiences:

57

We were transferred to Camp Bury and later to Camp Myerscough. But our friendship did not break then. Nearly every Saturday afternoon and every Sunday morning our friend Mr Bill Rawcliffe fetched myself and another pal (his name was Axel Tyden who went to Mr and Mrs Jack Wade) by car to his home and they brought us back to Camp Myerscough at Saturday evening and Sunday evening. So we were able to spend every Saturday afternoon and Sundays the whole day in our friends home with them. And later they lend us cycles and so we were able to drive by cycles to Oswaldtwistle. Some time my friends Mr and Mrs Rawcliffe went with me to a cinema and once when we were at Myerscough camp, we made a trip with the Sunday-school of Yorkstreet-Chapel to Morcumbe near Blackpool. Therefore we had to change our dress, because we were not allowed to go so far from the camp.

From Myerscough I went to Huyton near Liverpool and from there to Warrington. But I was still in contact with my friends Mr and Mrs Rawcliffe through writing letters. When I was discharged I came to Camp Wigan. And at one of the last days, my friends (the whole family) came to visit me the last time to say good bye. They came with many gifts which I should take home to Germany and after one or two hours the moment came where we had to take leave.

We all had tears in the Eyes. And so I have still to be thankful to my friends Mr and Mrs B Rawcliffe and to Miss May Aspinall and to Sheila Duerden for all the Goodness they gave me in a very hard time of my live. Also we have to thank your father, for he made it possible that I found so nice friends in England.

It was not surprising that Stanhill camp was to cease being used for German prisoners later in 1947. In fact the British government had stepped up its repatriation programme of German POWs from 3,000 a month to 15,000 a month at the end of the previous September. An announcement from Downing Street at the time had specified that priority should be given to prisoners who had shown a 'positive democratic attitude' and were therefore thought likely to play a useful part in the rehabilitation of Germany. Other criteria for rehabilitation priority included: length of time spent in captivity, exceptional compassionate circumstances, and people with industrial or other qualifications particularly needed by Germany at the time.

This programme of repatriation may have come about partly in response to public opinion that the process was taking too long for the sake of the prisoners themselves. The strain of prolonged and unnecessary separation from families was likely to undermine family life. The war in Europe had ended in May 1945 but a year later as well as the 338,000 German prisoners still in Britain there were also Italians, Austrians, Hungarians, Romanians and others. The organisation 'Save Europe Now' had been founded the previous year by Victor Gollancz, a well-known British Jew. It aimed to provide practical action and to act as a spur to government. Save Europe Now organised a petition to the Prime Minister, Clement Attlee, on 23 August 1946 urging the quickest possible repatriation of prisoners of war in Britain. The petition was signed by 3 archbishops, 55 bishops and other church leaders, 118 Members of Parliament, 76 Fellows of the Royal Society, a large number of heads of colleges and schools and many men and women prominent in literature and the arts.

1947 was by no means too early for the prisoners at Stanhill to be sent home. Christmas 1946 had been a comparably happy one, but to be going home was what they had longed and prayed for for years. Unfortunately they were largely unprepared for what awaited them in their homeland.

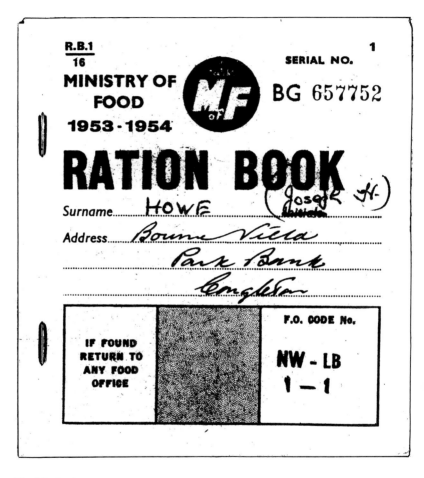

Fig 25: Ration books were to be issued in Britain until 1953.

4

Conditions in Europe

In Britain food was still rationed, and would remain so for a further seven years. Jumbled slogans at a Christmas party give a feel of the times:

Ivbrio vneetprs ttah nnksiig nelefig
(Bovril prevents that sinking feeling)

Tae rome fitur
(Eat more fruit)

Phos rayle dan doiva het uueesq
(Shop early and avoid the queues)

A review of food shortages in 1946 showed that people in the UK were obtaining about 2,800 calories per head per day. This was about 93% of their consumption before the war, and slightly above the current recommended minimum level to maintain full strength and efficiency, which was 2,650. But what of other parts of Europe? In France, Belgium, The Netherlands, Norway, Greece, Yugoslavia, Czechoslovakia, Italy, Austria and Germany, calorie levels were below 2,650 per person. As a result anaemia, rickets and malnutrition were not uncommon.

In Austria, which had been annexed by Germany in 1938 and was now occupied by our allies, the 'normal' rations available were sufficient for breakfast only. In August 1946 it was reported that there had been fresh meat only once in the

ROUND THE WORLD

The "Haves" and the "Have Nots."

Below is a table giving the civilian consumption levels of most European countries, the United States of America and the Dominions. A thick line is drawn through this table, marking the 2,650 calorie level, recommended by the U.N.R.R.A. Food Committee as sufficient to maintain full health and efficiency. This table shows the *quantity* of the food, rationed and unrationed, consumed in these countries during the three months, April to June, 1946.

CALORIES PER HEAD PER DAY FROM ALL FOODSTUFFS.

April—June, 1946.

	Calories.	Per cent. of pre-war.
United States	3,100	100
Canada	3,000	100
Australia	3,000	97
United Kingdom	2,800/2,850	93/95
Denmark, Sweden	2,800/2,900	90
France, Belgium, Netherlands, Norway (whole population).	2,300/2,500	75/85
France, Belgium, Netherlands, Norway (non farm population).	2,000/2,300	—
U.N.R.R.A. countries† (whole population) ...	1,700/2,400	60/85
U.N.R.R.A. countries (non-farm population) ...	1,500/2,100	—
Germany (4 zones) (whole population)	1,600/1,800	50/60
Germany (4 zones) (non-farm population) ...	1,250/1,600	—

†U.N.R.R.A. countries : Greece, Yugoslavia, Czechoslovakia, Italy and Austria.

Figures from the Second Review of the World Food Shortage, July, 1946, issued by the Ministry of Food and published by His Majesty's Stationery Office.

Fig 26: Figures showing inadequate food supplies in most of Europe, quoted in a booklet entitled 'Have You Thought What Winter Will Be Like

Now here are tables giving the approximate consumption levels of meat, fats and sugar. These tables show the *quality and variety* of the food. Again a sharp contrast is revealed and a thick line has been drawn between the " Have " countries and the " Have Nots." The people of the United States, Canada, Australia, Denmark and the United Kingdom have eaten during the past year from two to three times as much meat and fats, and from three to eight times as much sugar as the people of the U.N.R.R.A. countries and of Germany. Furthermore these figures are approximate as current import allocations for continental Europe may not be achieved in full.

MEAT (including bacon and offal) as carcase weight.		FATS (including butter) for edible and technical purpose (*e.g.*, soap).		SUGAR (Cane and beet sugar only).	
Actual lb. per head per year.	As per cent. of Pre-war.	Actual lb. per head per year.	As per cent. of Pre-war.	Actual lb. per head per year.	As per cent. of Pre-war.
Over 120 lb. :		*Over 60 lb. :*		*Over 80 lb. :*	
United States	120	United States	90	Australia	90
Canada	110	Canada	90	Sweden	90
Australia	80				
		50–60 lb. :		*60–80 lb. :*	
100–120 lb. :		**United Kingdom**	80	United States	70
Denmark	90	Australia	80	Canada	70
United Kingdom	80	Denmark	70	**United Kingdom**	70
		Norway	70	Denmark	60
80–100 lb.					
Sweden	110	*40–50 lb. :*		*40–60 lb. :*	
Belgium	90	Belgium	80	Czecho-slovakia	100
		Sweden	70	Belgium	70
		Netherlands	70	Netherlands	70
				Norway	60
60–80 lb. :		*30–40 lb. :*		*20–40 lb.*	
France	80	Greece	80	France	70
		France	70		
40–60 lb. :					
Czecho-slovakia	70	*20–30 lb. :*		*10–20 lb. :*	
Norway	60	—		Greece	70
Austria	40			Germany	40
Under 40 lb. :		*Under 20 lb. :*			
Yugoslavia	70	Yugoslavia	50	*Under 10 lb. :*	
Greece	50	Italy	40	Yugoslavia	70
Italy	50	Austria	40	Italy	30
Netherlands	40	Czecho-slovakia	40	Austria	10
Germany	30	Germany	25		

Figures from the Second Review of the World Food Shortage, July, 1946, issued by the Ministry of Food and published by His Majesty's Stationery Office.

In Europe This Year?' issued by Save Europe Now in the latter part of 1946.

past 18 months. For many months the Austrians saw nothing but bread and dried peas. The United Nations gave one supplementary meal a day to 91,000 children aged 6 to 18 in the capital, Vienna, but it was still estimated that half the children in Vienna were underfed. Warm clothing, blankets and footwear were lacking, especially for refugees arriving in Austria with no possessions. Shoe factories had partly resumed work but by June 1946 they were only able to supply sufficient shoes for the forces occupying the country.

In France there were riots over bread shortages in January 1946. A large minority were seriously underfed including students, adolescents, pregnant and nursing mothers and old people. Their sufferings during the occupation had led to a lowered resistance to disease. After liberation, many people succumbed to tuberculosis or suffered from decalcification of the bones, stunted growth and anaemia.

Greece, which was a poor country even before the war with 22% of the population having tuberculosis, suffered both invasion and civil war. Inflation wiped out life-savings. Flour distribution ceased in most parts of the country and hunger prevailed. Stunted and deformed children were familiar after-effects of famine reported by observers in August 1946.

In Poland, where the war had broken up countless families, malnutrition and tuberculosis were common. Potatoes were practically the only food to be bought in many parts of the country and potato soup was the main meal. The urgent need for beds, bedding, clothes, medical supplies and toys was reported, with of course the shortage of food causing the most widespread and acute distress.

What, then, were the conditions prevailing in Germany which the returning prisoners were to find? Germany had been divided at the end of the war into four zones. These were administered by Russia in the East, Britain in the north, the USA in the south and France (a small zone) in the west. Greater Berlin, although situated within the Russian zone, was also divided into sections, Russia administering the north east, Britain the north west and the USA the south west.

In October 1945, Field Marshall Bernard Montgomery had

made a statement about conditions in the British zone of Germany:

No-one need be under any illusion that the German people are getting off lightly. Only the bare minimum of food can be obtained. In winter, when temperatures well below zero must

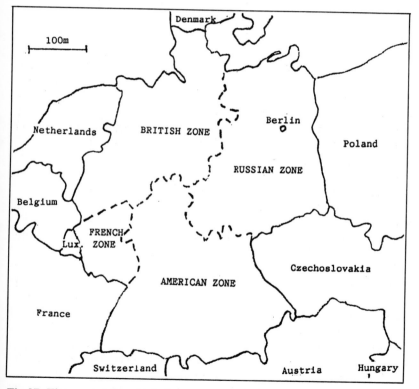

Fig 27: The zones into which Germany was divided in 1945.

be expected, there will be no coal for heating houses and the population will have to depend on stocks of wood they are being urged to collect. In large towns more than half the housing accommodation has been destroyed, and large numbers of people are living in cellars or impoverished shelters ... The damage to the railways and inland water communications had been so great that it is extremely difficult to move even what stocks of coal and food we have from one part of the country to another.

... I am aiming at a ration of 1500 calories per day, compared to the British civilian ration of 2800, but even this standard has not been reached in all parts of Germany owing to difficulties of distribution. To make matters worse the harvest this year is below normal, in some areas 50% below ...

If I were asked what was my main fear during the coming winter, I would say that it was fear of disease. I have over 20,000,000 people in the British zone, and I doubt very much if they have the resistance power to "see off" diseases such as influenza. I do not think we can stop such outbreaks, but we must be able to handle them if they occur.

The position turned out to be even worse than Montgomery had envisaged. Due to 'unexpected and unfavourable developments in grain supplies and distribution' the normal food ration in the British zone was cut to 1,050 calories per person per day on 4 March 1946. Where there was no possibility of supplementing these rations from other sources, slow starvation set in. The effects of this reduction were seen immediately. Absenteeism from work suddenly increased. Coal production fell in March from 182,000 tons per day to 150,000 tons. Men on the shop floor dropped at their machines and signalmen fainted on duty. Production in the steel industry fell between 10 and 20% by mid-1946. The repair rate for locomotives fell by nearly 30% between March and June. On 5 May, Mr Herbert Morrison, deputy Prime Minister, stated, 'We do not love the Germans, but their coal, which they cannot mine if they are starving, is vital to the economic reconstruction of Europe.'

The infant mortality rate in March was 104 per 1,000 live

births (as compared with 64 in March 1938). Pregnant and nursing mothers, although receiving more than the normal ration (2,139 calories instead of 1,050) were simply unable to support the demands on their constitution. By mid-1946 any domestic stores of food, which had helped to eke out rations for some families, had largely been used up.

In a mental hospital in Dusseldorf lack of food reduced patients 'to a physical condition so dreadful that it required an effort of will not to run away from the sight in horror' according to an observer writing in a Save Europe Now pamphlet. The state of nutrition had begun to deteriorate in this mental hospital in mid-1945. In June 1946 alone, 25 of the 700 inmates died of starvation.

Two out of every three people in Germany as a whole were described as having the opaque, yellowish, deadened skin and loss of weight typical of malnutrition. Apathy, listlessness, endless fatigue, stupor and collapse was the progressive outcome.

On 3 June 1946 a group of food experts from a tripartite nutritional committee, who had toured the British, American and French zones, reported 'large and positive evidence of malnutrition and physical deterioration among German civilians' in all three zones. They pointed out the 'serious condition of children and aged persons who had least opportunity for obtaining supplementary rations', and the 'reappearance of famine oedema which had disappeared in January but had again reached serious proportions in urban areas'. They referred in particular to the lack of vitamin B among children under thee years of age, the calorific deficiencies among six- to ten-year-olds, and the retarded or arrested development among those aged between ten and eighteen.

In July the ration in the British zone was said to have risen to 1,137 calories, but by 22 August the minister in charge of British affairs in Germany described the rations as still 'far below that at which health could be maintained'. Tuberculosis had assumed serious proportions in Hamburg (4,372 new cases reported in the first five months of 1946, as against 1,617 for the whole of 1945). There were twelve deaths from famine in Hamburg in the last week of July alone.

In addition to medical and economic repercussions from the March cut in rations, there were also social ones. People raided and stole from food stores and looted trains carrying supplies. There was a great increase in illicit trading and black-market activities. Demonstrations were reported in many towns: on 28 March 50,000 people gathered in Dusseldorf; on 1 April 10,000 took part in a hunger march in Duisburg. On 9 May 150,000 people staged orderly mass demonstrations in Hamburg and on 13 May 20,000 came together in Flensburg. In Remscheid reports were made that the ration level sank from 1,220 calories to 690 in a six-week period, and 10,000 people took part in a hunger march on 23 May. The food crisis was ascribed by British officials less to an overall shortage of food imports than to the effects of the severe winter and failure to obtain the scheduled collection of grain and meat from German farmers.

The situation in Europe as a whole in mid-1946 was summed up by Save Europe Now as follows:

> The general picture is of a world where millions are short of the primary necessities of life, where active cooperation of all nations is required in a great combined effort to alleviate suffering ... Meanwhile, however, those in distress continue to suffer, and it may be some time before the world-wide plans of international organisations can bring effective aid to all who need it. It is in the intermediate period that the work of voluntary agencies ... is of such significance.

In fact the crisis was to drag on throughout 1946 and 1947 and into 1948 when there were 24-hour strikes of workers in many German towns due to 'starvation rations'. The largest of these was a mass strike of all white-collar workers in both the British and American zones on 3 February 1948, estimated at a total of 2½ million strikers. To tackle the problems of hoarding of food and illicit trading, all the allied authorities brought in new measures in a so-called 'pantry law'. This required all private households, farms, shops, cafes and firms dealing in foodstuffs to make returns of their stocks by a given date. Questionnaires were distributed and offenders were liable to up to three years' imprisonment and heavy fines.

Relief agencies sent out teams with food supplies hard-won from the depleted world markets to help those most in need. They appealed for even small gifts of money and food which would 'save the lives of thousands of children and adults'.

This was the situation in which the prisoners' families were living, although the prisoners at Stanhill were unaware of its gravity. The repatriation for which they had yearned for so long was to be marred by these unimagined hardships. They were exchanging a certain level of security in a British prison camp for a life of deprivation and struggle at home. What could the ordinary British person do to help and how did the people of Oswaldtwistle respond?

5

Parcels for Europe

On 7 February 1946 the British Minister of Food, Sir Ben Smith, had told the Commons that there was a world food shortage. There was therefore to be a reduction of rations in Britain. The wheat content of bread was to be reduced to the 1942 level and bread would look darker. The butter, margarine and cooking fat ration was cut from eight to seven ounces per person per week. Sir Ben said that the biggest single factor in the situation was the need to feed thirty million German people for whom famine loomed, following the destruction of their agricultural industry in the war.

Despite these limitations on food in Britain the government decided later in the year to allow people to send rationed food in small parcels, weighing not more than seven pounds, to contacts in European countries. This news was announced on 3 December 1946. At first, all such parcels had to be sent via Save Europe Now in London. A postal order for one shilling and six pence or four shillings had to be sent in advance to this address for the necessary labels, the larger amount if the parcel was destined for a named person.

All food had to be in sealed tins and was listed in order of suitability as: tinned meat, tinned fish, tinned milk, dried eggs, flour, semolina, barley, oatmeal, macaroni, tinned beans and peas, chocolate and sweets, dried milk, dried fruit, tinned syrup, jam, honey, treacle and sugar. Also soap, soap flakes and rationed soap-powders could be sent. Parcels could only consist of 'rationed food, food on points, food on personal points and rationed soap, and must not include more than two pounds of any one article'. Unrationed food (such as coffee, cocoa, Horlicks, Ovaltine, cod liver oil, tinned vegetables and soup) was not allowed, presumably so as not to deplete supplies. Not more than one parcel a month could be sent from the same source to the same named person.

The people of Oswaldtwistle responded without delay. As one former prisoner recalled 44 years later:

A few weeks before Christmas when your father came to Stanhill Hostel he collected addresses of our families and requested the Church people to send parcels to our families because in Germany at that time just after the war food had been very, very little and was rationed. So my mother got a parcel for Christmas and also in the following months.

Even while Christmas preparations were being made, the *Northern Daily Telegraph* reported (on 17 December 1946):

Oswaldtwistle Methodists are planning to send Christmas food parcels to relatives of Protestant German prisoners of war at Stanhill Camp ... At present parcels, to be sent through the "Save Europe Now" scheme were having to be restricted to the families of 18 men who had attended the services regularly. Both food and money to meet the expense had been willingly given and the people of York Street Church were making themselves chiefly responsible for the gifts, which it was hoped to send not alone to the British, but also to the American and French zones.

As a result of this newspaper report my father received letters such as the one from Mrs Astin of Clayton-le-Moors: 'We tried to send the parcel from the post office but they could not accept it. I read in the press that you were sending parcels and wondered if I could send one through your efforts ... '

He also received the following letter from Mr J. Aspin of Blackburn:

Dear Sir,

It is with great interest that I read in tonight's "Telegraph" of the good work that you are doing for the relatives of German POWs.

The article in the paper seemed to be specially printed for my benefit, but perhaps I had better first explain.

In November 1945 a party of German POWs came from Bury each day to work on a new housing estate near my home.

I became very friendly with one of these, a young man of 19 years of age, whose home in Germany is in Koslin, Pommern, which as you will probably know is in the Russian zone.

He has had no news of his parents from the day he was called up in March 1944 up to the present. In April 1946 he was moved to a camp in Cumberland, and we wrote to each other regularly. He by the way having learned a good deal of English by taking lessons when in camp at Bury.

About three months ago he told me that he had applied to go back home to the British zone, and that I must not write again until I heard from him.

Well today, the very same day on which the article is printed I have received a letter from him in which he says that things are not so good in Germany, food is scarce, clothing also.

I, not knowing whether it is allowed to send anything to ex-German POW am wondering how I can help this poor lad, and then I open my newspaper and find the article about you and your Church.

This seemed to me to be an answer to my thoughts. Will you please let me know, what is one allowed to send to a friend in Germany, are there any formalities to be gone into etc.

Hoping that you will excuse my "nerve".

I am yours sincerely,
   Mr J. Aspin

One of the first prisoners to return home from Stanhill was Heinz Müller, the first translator of my father's sermons. He left Stanhill on 19 November 1946 and so missed the Christmas celebrations in Oswaldtwistle that year. My sister remembers him as a tall, fair-haired, blue-eyed and handsome man. His first letter from Germany to my father was written on 25

February 1947 from his home in Leipzig in the Russian zone:

My dear Mister Howe,

At first I want to say you that I already started writing to you once before and I'm definitely hoping I'll succeed today. But now back to the beginning. As you know I left Stanhill on the 19th November for Bury, the Base Camp. I was very happy, for we, that is my comrades and I, seven altogether all from Bury or its branch camps, had only a few days to wait before being sent to another Camp, near Bristol.

There at this registration camp we met about 1600 others, all ready to be sent home. We all impatiently hoped to be transferred to the next harbour, in this case Bristol, immediately for embarkation. I believe you know how impatiently men can be a short space before the fulfilment of their desires. But how easily one is deceived! We had to wait for about two weeks before our great day arrived, and instead of being embarked at Bristol, we were to go to Hull. That didn't make any difference to us, however. We were on our way home at last, and everyone of us was very, very grateful for it. For even those who hadn't spent such a long time behind the barbed-wire than I had to, now felt as if a very strong and powerful pressure was taken from us. Years of captivity went down behind us and a life of golden freedom, the most precious value man is in possession of, we were looking for. It took us only 24 hours to reach Hamburg. From there a special train, in a much better condition than I had hoped for. At least it was clean and even a little bit heated, a blanket was given to us for the night and off we went for Munster Lager. There we spent 3 or 4 days, got our English discharge papers and the money we had earned and not spent in England.

... Very, very slowly the train brought us at first to Erfurt and later to Leipzig, my home town. If I had thought I would be at home now, I very soon found out I was mistaken. By order of the Russian Authorities all people that are coming from the west to our Town have to be brought to special Separation camps for an undergoing of quarantine. It wouldn't have been so bad, if it hadn't been so cold, and many of us, now being in their home-town again after a long time of separation from their beloved, couldn't spent Christmas together with their families, but had to wait until December

74

30th before being allowed to go home. But last of all every one of us was on his way home and a very short time later reunited with those who were waiting for him since long.

Myself I found my father and my wife, though healthy but both of them had grown old, and are looking very much older than they actually are. Not only all our towns and villages are showing these terrible signs of the air war, but also the people, who are living in them. Leipzig itself is approximately 25 to 35 per cent destroyed and ... I'm very sure it will take us a long, long time to rebuild our towns. For there are so many others, formerly beautiful towns and villages besides Leipzig. Dresden for instance or Munich, that are in a much bigger scale destroyed than our town. Only to get rid of all the rubbish alone will take many years. Certainly there are many bands working on it, even women are helping, in our town more than 3000 of them are, even now, although it is very and uncommonly cold, working as masons or just clearing the streets and roads of the mess.

My dear reverend, one who hasn't seen these towns will never be able to imagine all the destruction which has been done the last five months of the war. I myself thought I could make me a picture because my folks had written to me so many details about it, but I have to confess I was shocked when I saw it for the first time with my own eyes. Therefore I consciously avoided those parts of the town where most of the destruction has been done ... Everything has to be done by hand. Has to be done by men who are hungry all the time and who very seldom are as happy as to have our own home or house, or even a heated room to call their own. For you got to know that all the towns besides those citizens who lost their flats or houses, have to shelter thousands and thousands of these poor people who came and are still coming from Poland, Czechoslovakia, Silesia, East-Prussia and so on, and so on. I believe Leipzig alone has to take much more than 100,000, and we already had a population of 700,000 inhabitants. Therefore everybody and everywhere places are crowded, people pressed together. In my house we had been living with four persons, and are now today 10. I myself don't mind about it, because a place must be given to these people to live in. But what's more this winter is extremely cold, since the 10th of December daily about zero, and coal naturally is rationed. We get about fifty pounds a month. That is the same with electricity and gas. One week you get electricity from about 6 till 2 o'clock at noon. The next week from 2 at noon till night. Gas is more difficult, we mostly do get it from 5.30–6.30 am. You may imagine how awful difficult it is for the housewives to cook our meagre meals. Everyone, man and woman, has to take a job, only wives who are attending more than two persons besides themselves, are free. All the factories are working 3 shifts, day after day and week after week, but nothing can be bought by civilians. Everything is manufactured for the Russian Government. In many cases the factories have been dismantled and transferred to Russia after the raw materials have been used up.

On the other hand the food problem is very bad. I lost quite a bit of my weight in the last two months since I returned from your country. Actually our rations haven't been very big at Stanhill, but it was much more and more substantial than these here. To draw a picture of the whole ration system ... you normally should get 14 ounces of bread, 17 ounces of potatoes, 1 ounce of meat or fish or sausage, 1 ounce of so called egg-white-powder (synthetic), ¾ ounce of sugar, and $\frac{5}{14}$ ounce of lard. Nothing else besides that. You can imagine how difficult it is for the wife to prepare something tasteful and on the other side to find a menu that brings a little bit of variety into the daily meals. Children and heavy workers are getting a bit more than that mentioned above. For instance, children with less than five years are to get 1 pint of milk and 1 pint of skimmed milk daily.

But that is the same with all the other necessaries of life. We are very lucky to get a permit for a pair of shoes, a pair of trousers, a stove or anything else. However, if we have been lucky enough to get the permit, you mostly aren't able to buy the stuff, because it actually doesn't exist. Let us take one example. I still had about 15 yards of cloth and tried to get 4 shirts made out of it.

Therefore I went to my tailor. He only was to glad to do it, because I had the material. But now here is where the bottle-neck lies, he got to have the yarn to sew them, and he got to have it from me, for he cannot buy it. But I cannot buy it either, for there isn't any left. There is nothing left. Everything gone, used up during the war and in the 2 years after, and there is nothing coming out of production for the civilian sector.

... But now is the end of today's letter. I think I may broach something to you and may speak freely. As far as I know it is now permitted to send food parcels from Great Britain to Germany and even to the Russian occupied zone once a month. You must know that I wouldn't ask you to help me if it wouldn't be necessary. But I only would be too glad and grateful, if you tried and would help me now by sending a parcel too and fro. I'm not asking for me but for my father and my wife.

... Therefore, my dear Reverend Howe, let me again tell you how thankful I still am for the fine kind of real Christianity you have shown me, during the time I was permitted to help you at your work. Please give my best wishes to your wife and daughters and all my English friends of your congregation today and always.

Yours

Heinz Müller

My parents despatched a parcel of food to Heinz and his family in response to this desperate request. Postal services to the Russian zone were slow. The parcel was to take almost four months to arrive. We discovered later that the time taken for a parcel to travel the 100 miles, within the Russian zone, from Berlin to Leipzig was sometimes as much as three weeks.

Meanwhile other requests were received, some from persons unknown, but even so addressed personally to my father.

Schleswig Holstein
British Occupied Zone
Germany
April 27th 1947

Dear Sir,

My wife and I have lost in the war all our fortune, our well furnished apartments with all our clothing, underwear, crystal, porcelain, silver, paintings, my library, and our existence too. It happened two years ago, owing to the violent air raid on Dresden, February 13th 1945. (Until this fateful day my wife for more than 30 years a member of Dresden Staats Opera, I was myself writer and lector.)

Our whole life, devoted only art and literature, has changed on a cruel manner. Now we are living in a poor room. In the winter we have had neither a stove nor fuel, and how awful and bitterly cold was the winter this year!

We have not enough clothing and, worst of all, not enough to eat. To say the truth: we are starving. My wife has lost her health, her life is in danger, and I am suffering from tuberculosis.

Sure enough, millions of people in Europe are now-a-days in the same situation, but how many of them have the great luck to obtain care parcels from abroad. Not so my wife and I, because we have neither relatives nor friends in Great Britain, USA or elsewhere in the world.

May I beg you to help us and to give our address, as above named, to some nobleminded men and women, to some organisation or congregation, who want to provide poor people in Germany with clothing and food? In any case I would be very grateful for your kindness.

Innumerable letters of the same kind, just so well founded and not less urgent, may reach you, and any hope to obtain an answer may be therefore in vain.

I hope nevertheless. I have lost all my fortune, but not my ideals, and not my firm conviction, that real and true humanity and Christian charity never will end in the world.

Yours truly,
Karl H. Greggersen

As well as being moved by this cry for help, my father was also puzzled as to how this gentleman had obtained his name and address. A clue lay in the fact that it was actually addressed to 'Mr Joseph H. Howe, Minister of the York Street Methodist Church, Oswaldtwistle, England'. Perhaps Herr Greggersen had been in touch with one of the prisoners who had attended York Street during his time at Stanhill. My father responded as follows:

Oswaldtwistle,
May 16th 1947

Dear Friend,

Your letter reached me a few days ago. I am wondering how you obtained my address; perhaps if you can write again you

78

will tell me. I should be interested to know.

Your story is a tragic one. Any sympathy we can express seems so little but I do express my sorrow that you should be in such a plight. We can only pray that you will be comforted by Divine comfort, and that your temporal needs may be eased by some kindness shown by friends and neighbours. At this distance, what help we can send seems trivial, but I have arranged for a parcel of food to be sent.

... Many in this country are concerned for the needs of your people, and we trust that something will be done to meet the needs on a big scale.

... From time to time we are able to hear radio broadcasts of music from Hamburg. When it is possible for me to do so, I listen to these, and am glad that in spite of all, there is a love of music and beautiful things among your people. May the time soon come when this will be fully revived and the terrible scars, effects of war, healed.

Until then, "courage".

With Christian greetings to your wife and to you.

Faithfully yours,

Joseph H. Howe

Our family could not respond to all such requests for parcels from our own rations, and the government did not permit unrationed food to be included in food parcels. My father therefore continued to ask members of his congregations for help, and in this case Miss Kathleen Pilkington volunteered. About two months later, news came that this parcel had arrived safely:

Schleswig Holstein
June 30, 1947

Dear Mr Reverend,

Sometimes miracles do happen. A few weeks ago I received your letter from May 16th in which you announced a parcel of food, and yesterday this parcel has reached us, the long time owing to the difficulties of transport.

My wife burst into tears, opening the parcel and seeing all the good things which we missed so long. Indeed the content of the parcel is really a very great help for us and I beg you from all my heart to tell the nobleminded donor, Miss Kathleen M. Pilkington, 105 New Lane, Oswaldtwistle how grateful we are for this wonderful gift.

I know that food is scarce also in England and therefore it may be not easy to give away milk, meat and so on. I take it with many thanks as an offering for us war-victims.

Certainly we will be comforted by Divine comfort, as you write, dear Mr Reverend, but there is no possibility for us that our needs would be eased by some kindness shown by friends and neighbours. We have no friends and our neighbours are very hard-hearted. So fortunate to be spared from all horrors of war and nothing lost, they receives even on the "running belt" care-parcels with food and clothing from relatives in USA. My wife and I, however, in a state impossible at describe only in a few lines, have neither relatives nor friends in England, USA or elsewhere in the world and therefore no help — strange irony of fate!

Very often, if she thinks I don't see it, she looks into the mirror. Indeed our appearance has changed. After so much and heavy blows our hair is grey long before the time. She is anxious to hide it before me. On vein. The war has put his atrocious signs upon our faces. Besides, before our frightful disaster she was always smartly dressed and many women envied her beautiful costumes and garments; now she looks like Cinderella. I believe that it is unnecessary to tell you what this means for my wife.

Don't be angry, dear Reverend, if I beg you to ask now or later some nobleminded members of your parish for help for my wife or me with clothing if possible. It is a cheering fact that so many of your countrymen and women are eager to give us Germans a helping hand and to help to feed and clothe us and to heal war scars; this gives me the courage to my request. My wife, of very feeble and tender constitution and undernourished is after so much troubles and privations we had to go through in a state of complete despair and will have without any doubt a total breakdown, both physical and mental, if there is no help with clothes before the beginning of the winter.

Sincerely, and with many, many thanks,
　　Karl H. Greggersen

The cold weather referred to in letters from Germany had

by no means passed Britain by. On 29 January 1947 readings were taken of 16 degrees Fahrenheit. Power-cuts were widespread. On 12 February Buckingham Palace, along with numerous other homes, was lit by candles and was described as 'an icebox'; the King paid a timely visit to South Africa. By 22 February snow-storms were covering the whole of Britain except the north of Scotland. Many main railway lines were blocked, despite the use of snow-ploughs, and many roads were ice bound. There were ice-floes in the North Sea, the English Channel and the Thames estuary. Between 4 and 6 March, snow-storms, said to be of almost unparalleled intensity, swept England and Wales, rendering journeys between the north and south of the country almost impossible. On 5 March a train took 21 hours to reach London from Manchester. The AA described the road conditions as the worst ever known. Some snow-drifts were 30 feet high, with houses and trees disappearing under them. Over 500 food lorries were stranded, 300 roads were blocked and 15 towns completely cut off.

Thousands of British and Polish troops, and German prisoners of war as well as civilians were engaged in clearing snow from Britain's vital roads. Prisoners at Stanhill helped with this essential work. At seven years of age I recall walking along the pavements of the main road through Oswaldtwistle with snow piled to a height well above my head on both sides. The winter of 1947 was likely to be the worst winter of the century.

This parlous situation was made still bleaker by a coal shortage. Both gas and electricity depended on the use of coal for their production. A national fuel crisis developed. It was announced in March that restrictions on the use of electricity in domestic premises were to last until October. However, it was still so cold in May that, because of 'the cold weather spell in the North', certain restrictions which were to have come into effect on 5 May were deferred until the fifteenth of the month. There was a grave shortage of coal throughout the summer and no gas or electric fires could be used in residential premises.

These experiences meant that people were very aware of the importance of adequate clothing. Coupons had been needed for buying clothes since 1941 and were to remain in use until 1949. However, the government decided to allow the sending of clothing parcels to Germany within certain limits. Second-hand clothing in parcels of up to 10 pounds in weight, without any letter, could be sent in a similar manner to food parcels. No food could be included but goods such as books, stationery, educational commodities for children, and most mending materials could be sent. Excluded were all cotton goods such as cotton thread, blankets, shawls, travelling rugs, napkins, pillows, bolsters, mattress-cases, quilts, counterpanes, sheets and tablecloths. No electric boiling rings or heating plates could be sent, or wire, nails or tacks of iron or steel, rubber tyres or tubes, military uniforms, firearms or ammunition. No money, cigarettes, tobacco, dangerous drugs, jewellery, vegetable seeds, rubber or leather soles, or postage stamps could be included.

Save Europe Now distributed guidelines on 'What you can do to help Europe', pointing out that Europe would soon be facing its third post-war winter of privation. It continued:

All over the continent, from East to West, thousands of people — many of them still living in camps or bombed hovels open to the wind and rain — are wondering how they will survive the hard months ahead, menaced by the accumulating shortages of food, fuel, clothing and shelter.

... Our clothes may be a little shabby, and our clothing coupons may have to last a little longer, but we have still enough warm clothing to keep out the east wind. We may have fuel cuts during the coming months, but coal, gas and electricity will not become non-existent as they did last year in many European cities and may again this year.

Because of the drastic conditions in Germany, German prisoners in Britain were given an option from May 1947 to remain in Britain when their time for repatriation came, as civilian farm workers, initially until the end of the year. Each individual case, however, was subject to approval. The farmer had to provide housing and work without detriment to British workers. By January 1948 there were 7,750 such workers.

Eventually food parcels could be sent direct from local post offices after being franked at a local food office, and larger amounts could be sent in crates to Save Europe Now. Some churches that had not had the opportunity to develop personal contacts with prisoners' families made good use of this method. It is on record that Kingsway Hall Methodist Mission in London sent more than 40 parcels through Save Europe Now in the first quarter of 1947. Clothing parcels of up to 15 pounds in weight, could be sent by post, or of any weight by road or rail to various relief agencies. The ban on sheets was lifted so that old sheets and towelling could be sent to Germany for makeshift nappies, which were in short supply in Britain and non-existent in Germany.

Intellectual starvation was also being recognised. Arrangements were made for books, pamphlets and periodicals 'by writers of good repute published this century, and particularly since 1933' to be sent via various organisations or to named individuals by post. Newspapers were not included in this list of approved types of publication: they would have been out of date by the time they arrived and in any case some newspapers were being published in Germany.

Many people in Oswaldtwistle were by now sending parcels to prisoners they had met at Christmas 1946. For example, Mr and Mrs Haworth kept in touch with Franz Winschuh, Fritz Herold and Werner Jungnichkel. They visited Fritz after he was transferred to Worthmill Camp in Bury, and Werner when he was at Stanley Park Camp in Blackpool where, as a cook and confectioner, he was responsible for food for the officers' mess. They sent food and clothing parcels to all three men after their repatriation. Franz lived in Essen in the British zone. It was more difficult to keep in touch with Fritz and Werner, as they both returned home to what had become the Russian zone, but some parcels did reach them.

Although Herr Heinz Müller also lived in the Russian zone he proved to be the most frequent and fluent letter writer, sending eight letters to my father from Germany in 1947 alone. He also kept in touch with prisoner colleagues and was thus able to write from Leipzig on 7 June 1947:

... It has been a big improvement as to the conditions of German POWs in Great Britain since Christmas ... They may visit their English friends, may spend their spare time in the homes of your peoples and are even allowed to go by train to other towns to see foot-ball games, movies or the theatre. How much would I have enjoyed these opportunities for hadn't I longed for them for a long time. I hoped so much for it, because knowing other people in their own surroundings, within their houses will give you a much better and properly understanding of their life, of their living together, their character as a whole, and I believe, I definitely believe, if men, if nations would understand each other in a better way, things would be better and easier for everybody.

... Let me say you, dear Mister Howe, how much I will always be remembering the days we have been working together, to find a common base for the two congregations, to form a mutual community and give them the understanding that both of them, English and German folks, have the same simple wishes, to live a happy life with their families and to respect the freedom and the individuality of the others ... I have to say that the only true Christians I met in all my life, I found in England ... I have been in most of Europe's countries before the war, in Africa and America, but I have very seldom found men who I would like to call a Christian. But in your country I certainly found quite a number of people who were willing to help and friendly, without asking or what is much more, definitely knowing that there would not be a reward. I got to say this to you sometime, and I'm very proud to know you, and would only be too glad to call you friend.

... I was so glad to learn that the men at Stanhill made toys for the Sunday School children, and especially that your own little girls had such a lovely dolls house ... I would appreciate it very much to receive some photographs that were taken at this event you have been writing about, may be you will be able to send them later together with some of the newspaper pictures. For the time being it isn't possible to get any foreign newspapers ... Our own newspapers are only issued to the sub-

84

scriber each other day, and there is no paper on Mondays at all. There is a critical shortage of everything ...

I was sorry to hear that you lost Paul Krüger for translation and Walter Schwarz too. The latter will be home by now, but Paul will be still in England, although within another camp. I hope you are doing well with Heinz Hermann. Now when there are only about 50 men at the camp your community will be very small, but all the better you will be knowing each of the men very closely. It is now approx one year that you are doing the work at Stanhill.

Half a year has already passed since I came home. Many things had to be learned again that had been forgotten during the many years of soldiering, this and that was completely new and uncommon to me. For worlds had been broken down in the meantime, ideas abolished, others brought to life again, what was good yesterday is bad today and on the contrary. It isn't all to the best. But is much better not to say too much about it. I really would like to read one of your wonderful newspapers, but we are not able to buy any in our zone. The only paper printed in English are the "Moscow news", that is published twice a week at Moscow, but it is only printed in English, it does not breathe the true spirit of an independent newspaper. You will also not be permitted to send any papers to me, we will have to wait for that too.

But now I have to thank you for your kindness by bringing some food-parcels on the way. We will very much appreciate it and value it. I'm quite sure we will find a way in the very near future to repay these costs. Please don't think I'm only asking for it because I believe it is easiest and cheapest way to get some food, But I'm quite sure of what I promised you and I got to help my relatives. As to myself, there is not very much to say. I'm not too bad off, I feel fine and healthy, even if I lost some weight. I'm working together with father and I'm happy to be reunited with him and my wife. Both of them have been enjoying your letter very much, which I translated to them. They are returning all your good wishes to you and your family, and they really hope they could meet you.

... Now let me conclude my letter. It brings with it our good wishes to you, your wife and your two little girls, to Mr Fred Hindle and all the other members of your congregation. May God's blessing be with you all the time and may he sustain you and me, who always will be your sincere friend,

Heinz Müller

Letters and parcels took time to arrive and some were lost en route. But eventually a food parcel reached Leipzig and the following letter was received from Heinz. The other people referred to in this letter are Heinz's wife's brother's family who lived two houses away at 26 Carl Goerdeler Strasse. His wife's brother was still a prisoner of war in France at this time.

Carl Goerdeler Strasse 22, Leipzig
June 22nd 1947

Dear Mister Howe,

Today I have to thank you very, very much, for I received your parcel. It arrived yesterday, and I must say, we had a great joy opening it and seeing these wonderful, tasty things you have been sending to us.

But there is still more to be said about this precious parcel. I sincerely believe that providence made it arrive on June 21st. And it couldn't have been coming on a better occasion, for this June 21st is my birthday.

Now, I think, you will imagine how much we have been delighted to get the package. Naturally it was the food we were so glad to have, that wonderful salmon, herrings, corned beef, jam, tea and the other delicious things. But, that wasn't the most important, decisive side, it was the love and understanding of our English friends and the willingness of true Christians, that was coming to me and into my home. Life looked brighter instantly for me, feeling the old mutual tie of friendship and having definite conviction not to be forgotten. I'm proud to say that this feeling and this conviction have been the finest and most valuable birthday present I got.

But it goes without saying that the contents of your parcel have been valued by the wife mightily. And she has been asking me to say you and your wife her heartiest thanks for your unselfish kindness, and the willingness to help. We upmostly appreciate it.

Especially for the coconut bar I want to thank you very much. It has been given immediately to my sister-in-law for her two little boys. The older, Thomas is three and the younger one Michael is about one and a half years of age. Both of them had never tasted chocolate, and being sceptical first, found it very tasting, and were dancing like wee-ravens, beating with their arms, shouting and happily laughing, when it was evenly distributed, in small pieces amongst them. The funniest thing happened afterwards, when Thomas having eaten his last bit of chocolate asked his mammy: Please, say, Mammy, when does Heinz have his next birthday, is it soon, isn't it? Isn't that wonderful, what do you think about the little fellow. I believe he and his brother, they have been very, very happy. And so are we, the other family, too. We have not tried any of your presents besides the tea and the condensed milk, yet. As to the tea, we were very eager to try it, for father and the wife have not had any black tea since the beginning of the war, and as to the milk it had to be used immediately, because the tin had been damaged and approximately $\frac{1}{3}$ of its contents had been run out, but fortunately the little hole had been shut by the milk again, and therefore we could use the rest of it, even after such a long time of being in a damaged tin.

The other food we got to save for the time to come. It will not be easy the next few months. I don't think you will be able to make yourself a picture of the hardship of the present food situation. The scarcity of food is now so grave that there is no bread and no potatoes at the black market to get. Normally both things could be bought by paying 200 times the original price of the article. But there is nothing left to be bought besides the food you are entitled to get on your meagre ration cards. I cannot imagine, how anybody will be able or can manage to live without buying additional things like bread, potatoes, vegetables, butter, some eggs, sugar and so on. But now it is really impossible to locate the first two items. And as to the others, most of the things you can get are brought across the border from the British and American zone. I definitely know that the people of these zones don't have more to eat according their official rations, but the Military Governments over there cannot be so rigorous, as the one we have, otherwise it would be impossible for the populations to be engaged in the black market in such a manner. Quite a lot of men are doing nothing else than working as black-marketeers within the British and American zone. In the Russian zone, that is impossible, because everybody, men up to 65, and women up to 60 years, are obliged to work and have to be registered at the ministry of work. Only by this registration and the several other stamps and things you are entitled to your ration card. There is a so-called house-warden and above this the street-warden which are to ratify that you are working and which are above all the political judges of your own life and deeds. And I believe it wouldn't be too advisable to have these men for enemies. It wouldn't add to your safety. But I hope time will come when I can speak more freely.

All of us, we only hope, that it will not be so far off that we will have a United Germany, without the borders within it, which are only a big hindrance and keep us in the rear. It is really impossible that Germany and Europe will revive again as long as the continent is still split in two halves, East and West distrusting each other. And in fact it isn't necessary because all people want to live in peace and freedom.

But now my dear Mister Howe, let me come to an end. There will be more letters coming to you I hope! Therefore I want to say goodbye for today, and to thank you again and again for your kindness and love. Pray give my and my family's best wishes to your people and to your community and let me assure you that my thoughts are very often with you all.

I'm always your sincere friend,
    Heinz Müller

The two small nephews referred to in the letter did not know their own father at this time. The older one, Thomas, was eight months old when his father left for the army and the younger one, Michael, had not been born.

It seems that when this letter was written in June 1947 the split between East and West was already being felt, though the division of Germany into Democratic Republic (East) and Federal Republic (West) was not to take place until 1949. No-one could have realised in 1947 that the lack of freedom Heinz was experiencing in the Russian zone would continue for over 40 years.

Leipzig became part of the German Democratic Republic in 1949. As we now know, the two Germanys were to be kept separate (with a dividing wall from 1961) until 1989. In fact it was a huge demonstration in Heinz Müller's own city of Leipzig on 9 October 1989 which helped to lead to the fall of the wall one month later. Whether Heinz lived to see these developments I have not been able to discover. It would have been heartbreaking if he had known when he wrote the above letter that the division in the country of his birth was to be so deep and long-lasting. At this time at least he had hope.

Here is part of Heinz's next letter in reply to one from my father:

Leipzig
9th August 1947

... You wrote as to the parcel that it seemed so little, but my dear Mister Howe you cannot imagine — and I really mean what I say — you cannot imagine what it does mean to us. See, I really do not like to complain always, but as things look now, it is very easy to see how life will be in the near future. In our newspapers we read daily that the ration system of western occupied part of Germany has broken down, that the workers of these zones refuse to do their share of work as to the insufficient food rations and so on. But they never say anything about our own miserable organisation of food stuff, clothing or coal problems. Just take one fact for instance. The butter ration. Our monthly ration consists of 10 ounces and there is no margarine, lard, oil or any other fat besides. Now on August 7th only $\frac{1}{3}$ of the July ration has been given to us, the second third will be issued in the course of the following week and the last third will be distributed beginning with the 12th August but not in butter, you got to take sugar, for there isn't any butter yet. Can you imagine there isn't any butter now, now my dear Sir, in August, when the meadows and pastures of our country and hills and mountains are green and the food situation, let me say the distribution of butter, should be most easily to be obtained, there isn't any butter in my country. And I wouldn't like to see the labourer who didn't want to work or at least to say so. I don't know, where he would spent his later days. And that is the reason why I always have my letters posted within the British zone to avoid the Russian censorship.

My dear Mister Howe I am deadly convinced that the coming winter will be the hardest and most severe the German people has ever seen since ages and that hundreds of thousands, maybe millions will starve and freeze to death before the sun will spend his vital warmth again next spring. One of our municipal hospitals has already been cleared of all other patients and nearly 700 typhoid cases have found refuge and have been isolated there. I now believe that your parcels of which you thought they seem so little — actually do mean so much to us. They are highly valued and treasured.

... the town had to naturalise more than 125,000 people coming from the Eastern parts of Germany, as East Prussia, that is now part of Russia, or Pommerania and Silesia which are now Polish, or from Poland itself or Rumania, Czechoslovakia where they or their ancestors had been living for ages. All these folks are coming without belongings, wearing rags, mostly without shoes not having the vital things we really need to exist. These people have lost all vital energy and instinct of self-preservation and are an actual danger for all other men and women in their struggle for life and their bare existence. It is only a matter of time till the others are inflicted too ...

Sunday School children in Oswaldtwistle had heard of the desperate shortage of clothing in Germany and of the British government's decision that clothing parcels could be sent there. They had the idea of donating clothing instead of fruit and vegetables at the 1947 harvest festival church services. My father mentioned this in his next letter to Heinz, who found time to write his reply on his 13th wedding anniversary, as follows:

Leipzig,
September 6, 1947

... Now will you please give my heartiest congratulation to your young people for the idea of bringing clothing at the coming Harvest festival Service instead of fruit and vegetables as usual. My German brothers will only too much appreciate it. For there is really a great need of everything over here.

... But now my dear reverend let me come to an end, for my wife is getting impatient. Today is our wedding-day, the 13th and she insists, and I believe she is only too right, that the whole day has to be dedicated to her.

... Will you please receive our very best wishes to you, your wife and your two little daughters, Pamela and Josey.

Sincerely yours,

Heinz Müller

My father's reply was written on 22 October and Heinz wrote again on 9 November, this time referring to the business that he and his father ran in Leipzig, a shop selling optical articles:

9 November 1947

... I am travelling every 3 or 4 weeks for about 6 or 7 days to Rathenow, a small town between Berlin and Stendal, and to Ilmenau, a still smaller town in the Thuringian forest and to Jena. The purpose of this travelling is to get more and better optical articles we can sell in our shop. For I don't know if you are actually conscious of this fact, the whole economy has been and is planned by the government. But to be content with these small shares would mean to be willing to cease to exist. Therefore I got to travel and to find more and better things to satisfy our customers and to make ourselves a living. In our case it is quite simple for in Rathenow and Jena the whole optical industry is concentrated. And within Ilmenau and a few small villages within its neighbourhood the thermometer industry is found.

But naturally travelling today in our country does not mean going from one place to another by the means of a well heated, clean and comfortable train or bus, oh no, just in the contrary. At first it is very difficult to get the permission to travel at all. Secondly, after you got your licence by the chamber of industry and commerce you are trying to get your ticket for a certain day to each point of destination. In my case there is only one to Berlin needing normally 4 hours to make the 100 miles. Sometimes it takes him several hours more and that will mean to you, that you will not be able to find any means of communication in Berlin for the tramway as well as the underground railway ceases to exist after 10 pm. Therefore you got to stay where you are, at the station. I don't want to exaggerate and to call a station a station, but in most places it is only a place where the station has been standing for the time it has been

91

bombed out. It would be the same exaggeration to call the comical monstrum you are travelling in, a railway-car. In the most favourable case you can call it a box on wheels. Last time I came from Rathenow I was travelling in a car without any benches or other arrangements to sit on, 2 big openings to allow the passengers to get in and out, but without doors, and with about 8 or 10 holes that formerly had been windows, but had now lost frames and panes. Naturally the cars are not heated and so you will be able to catch a first-hand cold.

... The day before yesterday your parcel containing 3 bars of chocolate, 2 tins of condensed milk, one beans with tomato juice, one with salm, one with livre paste and one with meat arrived and has given great pleasure to us. As for the chocolate the two little boys are already able to call it by name seeing it, in the contrary to the first few times when they had never seen nor tasted anything like that. I believe they really find it as delicious as the wife finds the other beautiful things precious ...

... The next time I will try to send you a few postcards of my hometown, The Leipzig as it was before the war, and a few pictures as it is and looks now. I think it will be quite interesting to you.

Interesting as Heinz's letters were to my parents, they arrived so frequently that it was difficult for my father to find time amid his busy life to keep up with the correspondence. Thus, Heinz's next letter began as follows:

Leipzig, Dec 20th 1947

Dear Mister Howe,

We have not heard from you lately. We definitely hope you and your family are well off.

... Today I want to thank you with all my heart for the wonderful parcel you have been sending to us. It contained nearly all the finest and choicest things one can think of. Especially the margarine did find the undivided interest of the wife and was found in best condition. I would be only too glad if you would transmit my utmost gratitude to the teacher who gave some of the gifts as you wrote to me. But especially I have to thank you and your wife for the grand things and willingness to share the little food you get with us.

92

Now winter has come to us and the whole country is covered with snow. But thanks to God it is not very cold. Only a very few degrees below zero. We really hope it will stay so for the coal situation is very grave over here. But if it will not get too cold we think we can manage. I have been able to buy some firewood additionally and so are able to have a nice little fire going.

There are only a few more days to go till Christmas and we will spend the holidays at home as usual. Christmas Eve will see us under a tiny little tree and as we were as lucky to get hold of a few candles we will be united again for the second time after my long absence. It was just one year last Sunday I came home. Even if there are no presents this year, for there is not anything worth to be bought, we will be happier than ever and grateful to Our Heavenly Father to be united and together again. Our thoughts will be with you when the shine of the Christmas tree's candles will brighten and our prayers will enclose all four of you who have brought so much loving care into our lives in the last year.

On December 7th I returned from an eight days journey to Berlin and Rathenow in time for my wife's birthday. I was so glad to be back for the voyage was terrible. On December 1st all fast trains within the Russian zone ceased to communicate. Therefore it took me nearly 9 hours to make the 100 miles from Berlin to Leipzig. Everything is coming to an end. From today the tramway at Leipzig suspend the traffic for there are no spare parts to repair the last cars that have been in use lately.

This afternoon we went to the opera to see Mozart's Zauberflöte (Magic Flute) and we really enjoyed this wonderful music. It is only a pity that the Opera now has to dwell in a former dancing-hall, for the actual former Opera House has been thoroughly destroyed as all the other theatre houses, too. But after all it was a wonderful event.

Now we are home again and the wife is preparing the Christmas cake. By this occasion she wants to tell you that she is using some dried prunes you have been sending some day, as substitute for raisins and that she is only too glad to have them.

... We want to give you a Merry Christmas and a happy New Year. Always your sincere friend,

Heinz Müller

93

During 1947 all the German prisoners had been moved from Stanhill. My father was receiving requests from many quarters to send food and other commodities to Germany. Some of them came from prisoners who had been moved to other camps in England, such as the rather inappropriately named Merry Thought Camp in Penrith. The prisoners had heard more details of the shortages at home in Germany and requested that parcels be sent to their relatives. For example:

Merry Thought Camp, Penrith,
Cumberland, 14 Sep 1947

Dear Sir,

About seven months ago I was on posting from Stanhill to Merry Thought Camp. Therewith the connections with you and your parish broke off. The fate of POW was to bear much easier by the Christian charity which you showed to me and my comrades. I am missing it very much. Up to date I couldn't get in touch with someone here whom I could ask a favour as I should like to beg you for.

Is there any possibility to arrange sending a parcel to my family ...

Yours very sincerely,
Josef Leidl

My father replied, promising that a parcel would be sent. This prompted further requests:

23 Sep 1947

Dear Sir,

Thank you very much for your letter. I assure you that I will not only always remember you but I shall think, speak, and work myself in real Christian spirit. I like to think at the several occasions at your parish particularly the past Christmas. Once more I shall be not at home at this feast.

Convinced of the fine spirit which you and your Parish people always showed I put up to you the request in my last letter specially with regard to the coming Christmas. Without doubt you are not indignant at me submitting also an address of a good comrade ...

Josef Leidl

Herr Leidl listed addresses for the Leidl family in the American zone and the Hösl family in the French zone. A Christmas card arrived that year from Josef Leidl signed 'Your sincere friend Josef', posted from Longview Lane Camp, Huyton, Liverpool. The envelope was one of those made from paper that had been a map. When unfolded, the inside of the envelope showed Britain's attempt at mapping some German town, with question marks over certain blocks of buildings.

Evidence of the sending and safe arrival of other parcels frequently came from other camps. For example:

POW Camp, Ashton in Makerfield,
Near Wigan, Lancs. 6 May 1947

... I have dear Sir a good message for you. The parcel you sent to my wife has arrived just 3 days before Easter. My wife and my children were very happy on receiving your parcel and they all express their warmest wishes and God's blessing to you. I also join their wishes, and especially thank all brethren and sisters of the parish. May God reward you for your good heart.

I always remember all the nice days and hours I was spending with you, and all the members of your parish. They all have always been very kind to me and therefore I shall never forget this in future. What this Camp concerns I musn't grumble but it cannot be compared with your place. Especially the God-Service I always used to attend in Oswaldtwistle I'm missing here. I was always pleased to listen to you when you were praying in Church.

... Now, dear Sir, I have to tell you that I can expect to be repatriated in a month's time (might be 1 month later). I am looking forward to seeing my family, for many years have past since I have seen them last time.

Once again accept my best thanks and give my kindest regards to all members of your parish.

I am yours sincerely,
Gustav Sonnenberg

Fig 28: The inside of the unfolded envelope from Josef Leidl's Christmas card, posted in Liverpool, 23 December 1947. It was made from a British attempt at a map of some German town.

96

A Christmas card arrived from Gustav and his family in the Russian zone, dated 8 December 1947.

Two of the prisoners who had become friendly with Mary Clarke and her father at Christmas 1946, Ernst Pensch and Willi Lubecke, had requested that parcels be sent to their relatives. News of the safe arrival of these parcels came in May 1947:

> Merry Thought Camp, Penrith
> 14 May 1947
>
> Dear Sir,
>   You will be surprised to get a letter from two men who were often in Mount Pleasant and York Street in Oswaldtwistle. Do you remember Willi Lubecke and Ernst Pensch? ... Now I will let you know that Willi's wife and Ernst's mother received a packet of food which have been sent by your friends of Mount Pleasant. Willi's wife and Ernst's mother were very glad when they got the packets and thank you very very much for the gifts of food. Willi and Ernst also thanks for the sending of food.
>   Please forgive me when I made any mistakes.
>   With the best wishes,
>   Yours sincerely,
>   Willi and Ernst

My father replied to this letter and asked them to let him know when they were due to go home. This simple suggestion was taken very literally and resulted in several letters, such as one in June saying, 'Our repatriation is moved back. Our people at home are waiting for us and we cannot go and help them. It was a nice time when we were in Stanhill and the people were friendly to us always. We should like to stay in Stanhill for the rest of our prison life'.

September brought another letter from Willi and Ernst, 'Just to let you know we are still all right. Today Willi got orders to go home to Germany on 23 September. We have heard from Miss Mary Clarke you are on holiday. I hope you have had a good time'.

Heinz Müller heard from my father of Willi's repatriation

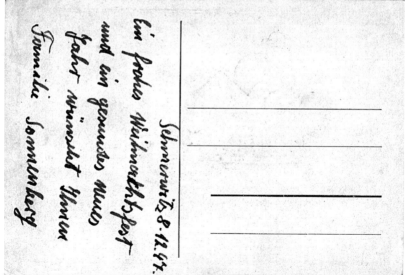

Fig 29: The Christmas card received from Gustav Sonnenberg and family, Christmas 1947.

and wrote, 'That Willi Lubecke has already gone back home is good news, for he was a good man, who really longed for his family and will now be very glad to be home'.

In October, Ernst wrote to say that he was to return home on 12 November. Next, there was a card dated 13 December written in Weddingen in the British zone:

I went by ship from England 29 November about three o'clock in the afternoon and arrived in Holland twelve o'clock at night. Then we went by train from Holland to Munster Lager in Germany. We arrived in Munster 30 November 8 o'clock at night. I left Munster Lager on 2nd December and was home 8 o'clock at night. It was a nice feeling to be a free man and going home after a long time. I was very pleased when I came to my village and my mother was very happy when I entered the house. She was surprised because she didn't expect me so soon. I feel very well now. My mother and I wish you and your family a Merry Christmas and a happy new year.

    Yours sincerely,
    Ernst Pensch

Even into 1948, requests for help kept coming. A letter written in German arrived in March 1948, which translated read:

Munster, British zone 6.3.48

My very esteemed Rev Howe,

Please allow me to write a few lines to you. I have been here with my parents in our new homeland since the 19.12.47. They have been here for the past two years as refugees after being driven from their home. I have been able to get work nearby, but it is very hard because one is thinking of "Home" all the time. My thoughts are very often in Stanhill and Oswaldtwistle where I had the pleasure of spending many happy hours in your company. It grieves me that I cannot go to church here as I haven't anything to put on. I only have the suit in which I returned from England and I have to wear that for work.

As you, Rev Howe have been so good to us, allow me to ask you a favour. Would it be possible to obtain a pair of trousers and a jacket for me? I sincerely hope you can, as it was impossible for my parents to bring anything along with them because they had been robbed by the Poles. And here these things are unobtainable.

   With friendliest greetings I remain
   Your thankful
      Gunter Krause

How my father would be able to send clothes without knowing something about the size of the man remains a puzzle! Whether he did respond we shall never be sure.

Fifty years later we now know that thousands of German families received parcels from Britain during this period. As one writer put it, ' ... they came out of the blue from the former enemy ... waves of unexpected mercy and hope'.

6

Continuing Friendships

1947 must have been a busy year for the postman in Oswaldt-wistle. Many letters and cards arrived at our house, not only asking for food and clothing, but sending thanks for recent friendship or simply wishing to be remembered. For example, Leonhard Luba wrote from the camp in Bury, Lancashire, on a printed army postcard intended for German prisoners' messages home. This one simply read: '30.3.47 Dear Pastor Howe, I wish you a joyful Easter-feast, and God's richest blessing. With kind regards, Leonhard Luba.'

Another unexpected letter came from Rev. Norman Dando, Methodist minister in Bedford, regarding a German Pastor who had spent a short time at Stanhill camp. It read as follows:

18 June 1947

Dear Mr Howe,

Yesterday afternoon I received a call from a German POW chaplain, Pastor G. Holthaus. Among other things, he said he was anxious to send greetings and thanks to you and your people for kindness shown while he was in Oswaldtwistle.

He is now in a camp at Clapham, near Bedford. I undertook to write and send you his message as he seemed diffident about writing on his own behalf. In case you care to have details of his present address, here they are:

G Holthaus 652796
POW Camp 278
Clapham
Nr Bedford

With kind regards and every good wish, I am,
Yours sincerely
Norman E Dando

By May 1947 only 50 men were left at Stanhill camp and by mid-September all the German prisoners had been moved to other camps or sent home. Many were keen to remember and keep in touch by correspondence with the friends they had made.

It was perhaps not surprising that Walter Schwarz was one such. He had visited our house not only on Christmas day 1946 but on several other occasions afterwards. His experiences as my father's helper had made a deep spiritual impression on him. His family had been forced by the war to move from their home in Silesia (on the borders of Germany, Poland and Czechoslovakia) to Oesselse, 12 miles south of Hannover in the British zone of Germany. My father arranged for a food parcel to be sent to his parents. On being freed from Britain in May 1947, Walter went to his parents' new home. He immediately made contact with his girlfriend who lived some distance away. Although their living accommodation in Oesselse was cramped, Walter's girlfriend went to stay with them for a while. As well as remaining in touch with my father, Walter wanted to explain something of his spiritual experiences in England to his local pastor. The Lutheran pastor in Oesselse was away from the area on holiday at the time of Walter's repatriation, as his first letter to my father shows.

Oesselse, British zone
15 June 1947

Dear Mr Howe and family,
I think you will be waiting for a letter from me. In the last time I was very busy and my girlfriend was come to us and so I could not find time to write a letter.

It was May the 5th whom I'm arrived at my home. Our family was very happy and glad to see me after such a long time. The pastor in our small village has holidays and so I could not have a word with him, but I like to do it in the

102

coming week.

For the food which you and your congregation has given to me, shall I say to you on behalf of my parents thank you very very much.

We are all well and I hope the same from you and your family.

With kind regards to you, your family and mother in law,

Yours very sincerely,

Walter Schwarz

It seems that Walter had not forgotten my grandmother who was staying with us when he was our Christmas day guest!

The Lutheran pastor to whom Walter eventually talked about his experiences in England was Pastor P. Gäbler. He had been a missionary in India for 14 years and his five children had been born in India. However, when war broke out he and his family were interned in camps in India simply because they were German. The internment lasted for seven years. Pastor Gäbler could therefore empathise with Walter's life as a prisoner. The following month brought a letter to Oswaldtwistle from the Pastor, a letter showing how the war had made its impact in various ways on his life and the lives of many members of his congregation.

Oesselse, 7-7-1947

Dear Mr Howe,

The other day I had a long talk with Mr Schwarz, a member of my congregation who returned two months ago from Prisoners of War Camp in England and brought me greetings from you. He was full of what he had experienced during the long years of his captivity, and particularly he was happy to have found Christ and to have been invited so often to your house. He finds, of course, conditions here in Germany worse than he expected, but he is facing the situation bravely. He asked me to tell you that he wants to thank you for the love and fellowship which you and your family and your congregation members have shown him and his comrades, and he says that he prays for you all with a very grateful heart.

Indeed it gives me very great joy to write this letter to you. During the long years of work in India as a missionary of the

Fig 30: Pastor Gäbler with his children Vroni, Micky and Christoph, taken in an internment camp in India in 1944 or 1945.

Leipzig Evangelical Lutheran Mission (since 1925) I met a number of missionaries belonging to the Wesleyan Methodist Mission in South India (Trichinopoly, Madras and other places), and I shouldn't be surprised if you knew some of them as eg the Rev. E.R. Richardson who returned from India 10 years ago, or Miss Holinshed who belonged originally to Burma. They were really very good friends of ours. Owing to the war we were, of course, interned and I spent with my family almost 7 years in several Parole Camps. We hoped fervently that we would be released like some of the other German missionaries, but we were disappointed. Instead we were repatriated to Germany and arrived here at the close of last year. I had the good fortune to find a vacant pastorate with a parsonage in which 3 rooms became empty owing to the transfer of my predecessor, and I could settle down here with my family. We had no furniture, plates, cups or anything like it; but the members of the congregation lent us what we needed most, I borrowed a few bulbs from the church, and then we were able to manage. As we were without provisions for the winter and had no potatoes, it looked rather bad for us, but there, too, the congregation helped us, and we have much reason to be grateful to God and man. Our eldest daughter went last year while we were still interned to America where she is a student in Berea College, Berea, Ky.; a member of the American School staff in Kodaikanal, South India, arranged for her to be invited by a fine Christian in America, a rather well-to-do gentleman, to go there and study and live for 4 years at his expense. How happy we are about that, though it is hard to miss her for such a long time. Our second daughter, 17 years old, helps my wife in the household here. Our two boys, Christoph and Michael, (9 and 7) go to the village school here, and Veronica (5) to the Kindergarten. We came here in the midst of the terrible winter and were more than glad when spring time came. I find the people of my congregation (1500 souls, half of them displaced persons and refugees from the east of Germany) rather open for the Christian message: many of them have gone through terrible experiences; they have lost loved ones, their houses and possessions and have become as poor as beggars. Their health is undermined, and most of them are undernourished and fall easily sick. Only yesterday when addressing a missionary meeting and speaking about India I read out Matth. 9.35sq; but it struck me anew how true it would be of Germany to say what the text says about Palestine at the time of Jesus: "When he saw the multitudes, he was moved with compassion on them, because they fainted, and were scattered abroad, as sheep having no shepherd." Really, God's hand is heavy upon us all, and we pray that many may hear His voice and turn to Him. To be a minister of Christ is such times among such people is a heavy task, but a great privilege too.

Yours in Christ,
P. Gäbler

Next came news from Walter again, telling of his forthcoming marriage:

Oesselse, 18-7-1947

Dear Mr. Howe,
For your letter which filled me with great joy I thank you

105

most heartily. It is very nice to hear from a like-minded dear friend, and to hear also about the life and the work of a congregation which became for a year my second home. I am deeply interested in what is going on in your parish as we were permitted to take part in the meetings to such a large extent and became acquainted with very many friends.

I have spoken with our pastor here and have given him your address; I am glad he wrote to you; he showed me also your reply.

If nothing interferes I hope to have my wedding in September. We are going to celebrate it, of course, in a very simple manner in accordance with present-day circumstances, but that is not the most important thing. We have only one wish: that God may give us His blessings for our married life. It would be, of course, a very special joy for my fiancee and myself, if it were possible for you, dear Mr. Howe, to conduct the wedding service yourself, but it is a pity that the distance is too great.

My brother is at present still sick and will have to spend yet another 4 weeks in hospital. My parents and my little sister and Ruth enjoy very good health which I can say also of myself.

Since 13th June I have started work again in my old profession, and I like it well.

For the greetings of your brother-in-law and his family many hearty thanks! I wish him a speedy recovery. May I request you to remember me to him and his family.

I remember still very often your two daughters; they gave me much joy when I was still in Stanhill. I have often spoken about them to my own little sister. I wish Josey and Pamela good success at school.

I was quite surprised to hear that there were no prisoners of war left in Stanhill. But I am glad that you have taken over the cross and the Bible, because it is firstly well taken care of and secondly it is a reminder of our common work under God's Word.

Will you and your dear family and your mother-in-law accept my parents' and Ruth's and my own very hearty greetings.

Greeting you once again,
Your friend
  Walter Schwarz

The greetings my father had sent to Walter were from my uncle and his family, my mother's brother, relatives whom Walter had met at our house at Christmas 1946. As a Methodist minister in London during the war, my uncle had lived through the traumatic conditions of the blitz, which had affected his health. The war had taken its toll in many ways.

Losing no time, Walter and Ruth were married on 14 September 1947. Because of the many refugees and resulting overcrowding in Oesselse they were not able to obtain permission to live there and had to seek accommodation elsewhere in Germany.

My parents sent a food parcel to Pastor Gäbler and family, and about the same time it seems that I also wrote a letter to the Pastor's children, although I have no recollection of it now. I had recently had my eighth birthday. In return came a further letter from Pastor Gäbler, dated 5 November 1947. Enclosed with this letter was a neatly handwritten letter to my sister and me from Ulrike, the second of the Gäblers' five children, aged 17:

Oesselse uber Lehrte
Bez. Hannover
Nov. 5th 1947

Dear Josephine and Pamela,

We thank you very much for your lovely letter Pamela. How nicely you can write, and you are only eight years old. I must write for my little brothers and sister, as they can't write English. Christoph used to be able to write English in India but now he has forgotten it as he has to concentrate on German very much. But both the boys understand English, of course. In India they had friends among the sons of a Rajah. It was very nice of the government of India to allow them to leave the camp yearly for some months in order to visit them. It was also very kind of the Government to allow me to study in an American school on the hills in South India, together with my older sister Lore. This was an American missionary school, and our nicest memories are connected with it.

It was a great disappointment for us all to have to leave India because India is our home and we've lived there ever since we were born. My big sister and I spent one or two years in Germany when we were on furlough last. We are glad that we have found a parsonage in a country place. Oesselse is north of the Harz mountains and south of Hannover.

We keep some rabbits and some chickens and it's my job to feed them all. We also have a little Dachshund puppy, the long-haired type, and her name is Topsy. She's almost four months old and gets into all the mischief she can possibly get into. Best of all she likes to chase our chickens and make them fly over the fence to the neighbor. Vroni (Veronica) loves to carry Topsy around all over the place. She's five and a half and gets into just as much mischief as Topsy.

Please tell your parents heaps of thanks for that super parcel which they sent a while ago. We have just finished the delicious bacon tin and Topsy for her part cleaned it out with a couple of big licks. The bacon served us for many meals.

Love from us all,
Ulrike

The accompanying letter from Pastor Gäbler brought news of difficulties and deprivations, good news of Walter's wedding and also a request for help.

(20a) Oesselse, Post Lehrte, British Zone
November 5, 1947

Dear Mr Howe,

This is to thank you most heartily for your kind letter of 22nd July and, most of all, for the parcel which you sent us. You should have been present when we unpacked it! The children were standing by our side, and every tin etc was greeted with shouts of joy. It was very kind of you to remember us in this way though we are strangers to you, and we are very grateful to you for your great love. The things you sent us are a very real help and we enjoy them greatly. May God reward you and your dear ones!

My children were very happy about Pamela's letter. Ulrike has written a reply which I enclose. We are glad to know something about your family and it would be nice if we could remain in contact. Our children did not quite get accustomed yet to the climate here and are often down with colds. My wife too is not quite well — no wonder after the long years of internment and the difficulties we had to go through. Our three smaller ones have recently a spell of jaundice; Christoph and Vroni got through fairly easily, but Michael had a very serious attack and went into a coma; we had some anxious days and feared that he would die. But God heard our prayers and restored his health: he is still rather weak. We hope we will be able to send him for a while to Sweden so that he may become strong again.

You might have heard from Walter Schwarz that his wedding took place on September 14. I had the joy to officiate on that occasion. I took as a text for the wedding sermon Rom. 12.12 and referred also, in the course of it, to your letter and said that you at Mount Pleasant and York Street Churches wished to convey your good wishes to him and his wife and remembered them in their prayers. In the evening I went with my wife to the place where they are put up — a tiny little room where they and their relatives were gathered, and stayed with them for an hour. It is a real joy to be with such friends who are earnest Christians. Unfortunately, they are leaving this week for Quorum-Braunschweig where they are going to settle down. With all the overcrowding of houses, he was unable to obtain permission for his wife to reside here, and after much worry he was glad to find a place near Brunswick, for himself and his wife. We shall greatly miss them both. But as his parents will remain here, I hope we will meet occasionally again.

On account of the scarcity of coal, often in the evenings the electric light is switched off, and we all have to sit in darkness. Candles are practically unobtainable. Last week there was a prayer week for the prisoners of war, but one evening the service couldn't be held because there wasn't any electric light. A few days ago some kerosine oil was distributed, and we got two bottles of it, one for church use and one for our own private use. But we don't have lamps or lanterns to make use of it. I wonder if you could send us a small hurricane lantern together with one or two spare chimneys, and a tiny bedroom lamp with a small round wick? That would be a great help in the church and home. We can't even buy candles for the altar! Thus, most churches in Germany are without them now, as our church is.

You ask about English newspapers. In Hannover or Hildesheim (they are our nearest towns, about 12 miles from Oesselse) one gets occasionally one — but they are difficult to obtain.

I know Rev. Paul Rangaramanujam personally; he is a fine Christian and also a good speaker: your church can be proud of him.

And now I send you and your dear ones hearty greetings from my whole family.

Yours gratefully,
P. Gäbler

My father managed to send a hurricane lamp to Pastor Gäbler, as requested in his letter, and also two smaller lamps, with the help of the World Council of Churches Ecumenical Refugee Commission.

Next my father wrote to Walter and Ruth at the time of their wedding, but the problem of where to live had caused them great difficulty. When Walter found time to reply, he signed his letter for the first time, 'Walter and Wife', and enclosed a photograph taken on their wedding day. Here is the letter:

Brunswick, Nov 13 1947

Dear Mr Howe,

I sincerely hope that you will not mind my having kept you such a long while without an answer to your kind letter. It was, however, quite impossible for me to write you at a sooner date, as I always was on the way for an abode. Please accept my heartfelt thanks for your kind lines.

My wedding took place of September 14th with my parents and it was very nice, considering the actual hard conditions of life. I herewith beg to transmit my and wife's heartfelt thanks for the good wishes of yours and of your congregation, which we received through our clergyman Mr Gäbler. We are sending you a small souvenir in remembrance.

You will hear from me again with my next letter.

Our kindest regards to you, your family and all relatives.

Yours
Walter and Wife

Fig 31: Walter and Ruth Schwarz, who were married 14 September 1947.

The 'souvenir' was the photograph. Walter and Ruth wrote again as promised in the new year. They were staying temporarily with Ruth's parents:

Braunschweig
15.1.1948

Dear Mr Howe,

For the loving Christmas greetings of you and your family I thank you, also in my wife's and my relatives' name, most heartily.

We spent Christmas very quietly. Often I thought of the previous year when we POWs for the first time had the privilege to contact English families and make visits. I shall remember that always with joy. Now it was a great joy for me after seven long years to be reunited with my dear ones. This joy would have been even greater if we could be in our own

111

homeland, Silesia. But I still hope that once upon a time we shall return there.

Now something about my new home. At present we are still staying together with my parents-in-law, but soon we are going to have separate quarters. We are put up in former army barracks of the "Luftwaffe" which were partly destroyed during the war and which are being rebuilt in order to provide quarters for refugees. The men who work here are provided with living rooms, and since I was not able to get accommodation in Oesselse, I shifted to this place. It took me a lot of running about till everything was arranged for; I had to run from one office to another.

We only hope that the new year 1948 is going to bring some relief and improvements.

Let us pray to God that He may let rest His rich blessing in this year upon all countries and nations.

With very hearty greetings to you, your family and your mother-in-law.

Your friend,
Walter and Ruth

Next, news arrived of the parcel to Pastor Gäbler containing the lamps:

Oesselse, Post Lehrte
Bez. Hannover
British zone, Germany
13-4-1948

Dear Rev. Howe,

I feel troubled in my mind for not having written to you for such a long time. Sickness in my family (one of our sons, Michael was severely ill with meningitis from which he recovered wonderfully and the other children were also frequently ill) and pressure of work in the congregation delayed my doing so. But now I want to thank you most heartily for your two letters of Dec. 15th and Jan. 23rd as well especially for your parcel. It was very kind indeed that you sent us the hurricane lantern together with the two beautiful night lamps. The latter are in perfect condition, but the 2 glasses of the hurricane lantern were unfortunately in 100 pieces, so that we could not use it, spare chimneys being unobtainable here. Thank you very much for remembering us so kindly. If you should find it possible to send us some time spare chimneys, it would be probably better to pack them in two separate small card-board boxes and both in a bigger box so that they can't be damaged. But now, when the summer approaches, we don't have to fear any more the cutting off of the electric supply; that will be probably the case when autumn approaches.

We read with great interest all that you wrote about your family as well as about your work, particularly in connection with the prisoners of war. This piece of Christian work is certainly something that the prisoners will never forget. We ourselves will always cherish the memory of the friends in India, both English and American who during our time of internment showed us that the Una Sancta is something very real and that in Christ there is no difference in race or anything else. I welcome very much the idea that you and our congregation should draw together and share with each other their own experiences. I will put the matter before the elders of my congregation and let you know about the result. The matter needs thought and prayer, as the villagers here are slow and reserved whereas it is easier in your own case; your congregation members have had already many contacts with Germany through the prisoners of war whom they have helped in so many ways and with whom they have come into personal contact. It is really a great thing that your people are stretching out their hand to us, and I trust that the response on our side will not be lacking.

I did not know yet "Guide me, O Thou great Jehovah ...", it is a fine hymn! "Jesus seek! with promise abounding", on the other side, is very well known and is found in practically all German hymn-books.

Now and then I meet Walter Schwarz when he comes to see his parents here in Oesselse. He is now looking forward to the arrival of their baby. He has settled down in his new place quite well, and after he has overcome the initial difficulties which the starting of a new household means in the present-day times in Germany, his life will be easier, I trust.

We hope to be able to send our daughter Ulrike and our son Christoph in the near future for a few months to Sweden where they have been invited to go. As Michael is rather weak, the Doctor advised us not to send him off to a distant place all by himself, but rather to find a place of recreation nearer by. We plan to take him along to Tübingen in the South of Germany where we plan to go in the summer for a month.

With our best wishes to you all, and with many thanks,

Yours in Christ,

P. Gäbler

Other letters passed between Pastor Gäbler and my father. One written in May 1948 refers again to my father's suggestion that the two congregations in Oesselse and Oswaldtwistle should make contact with each other.

I placed the matter of getting our two congregations into a closer contact before the representatives of my congregation. They welcomed the idea very much, and one of them in the meeting was appointed to start corresponding with your people. I translated your letter of Jan. 23 into German and await now his reply which I shall have to translate into English. But as he is a farmer who is rather busy on his fields it may take a little while till he gets the letter finished ... I expect to go next week on a month's holiday to Tübingen; I hope I will get the letter of our Church Elder there and pass it on to you from there.

I have no evidence as to whether anything developed from these ideas. Perhaps the necessity for translation of letters in both directions, which seems to have fallen to Pastor Gäbler, might have been a stumbling-block. Walter and Ruth Schwarz settled in Braunschweig where the last my father heard from them was that they were expecting a baby.

Christmas 1947 could not pass for many without remembering Christmas 1946 in Stanhill. Christmas cards were received at our house at Christmas 1947 from: Heinz Hermann in Herne, British zone; Paul Krüger who had been the camp interpreter, and had returned home on 18 June to Thuringen, Russian zone; Walter and Ruth Schwarz, then living in Braunschweig; Karlheinz Hösl, still in Penrith camp; Gustav Sonnenberg and family, Russian zone; Josef Leidl who had moved first to Penrith and then to Huyton camp; and Hans Motz and Rudolf Weiss, Bury camp. Some cards were accom-

Fig 32: Christmas card received in 1947 from Hans Motz and Rudolf Weiss.

panied by letters such as the following:

Bury POW camp
21.12.47

Dear Mr Howe and Parish,

Maybe you are wondering about to get a letter and Christmas Greetings from your German friends. But we cannot forget the time we spend in Stanhill and the hospitality we got in Oswaldtwistle.

So we like to write few lines to you, because we expecting to going home in the end of January. We are looking forward till the day is coming.

All the best wishes, Sincerely yours,

Hans Motz and Rudolf Weiss

Letters received from prisoners who were still in Britain at Christmas 1947 do not mention hospitality in homes at that time. It is known, however, that at Christmas 1947 prisoners in camps in various parts of the country were welcomed into private homes. My father's stepsister wrote from Northampton:

Fig 33: Christmas 1947 at "Waterloo House", Moulton, Northampton. My father's stepsister, Florence Pebody, third from left; Josef, a Romanian tailor, in the middle; and Willie, a German farm worker, on the extreme right.

We had a lovely Christmas. Had two nice chappies, one was a Rumanian named Josef. He is the tailor in the camp. The other namely Willie works on the farm at the back of us ... We had a Christmas tree and there were presents for all including the prisoners ... Everybody departed about 11.30. The prisoners had to be in by 1 o'clock and they had to walk back to the camp at Boughton. They seemed very grateful and Ann and I were so pleased we had them. Josef sent a New Year's card. We thought that was very nice of him.

Heinz Hermann was one of the prisoners who had helped my father while at Stanhill. After Walter Schwarz left the camp, Heinz helped with translation and on one occasion spoke in German in a church service. He had written from Penrith camp in September 1947 to say he was starting his journey home the following day:

Penrith, 5.9.1947

Dear Mr Howe!

I suppose you will have heard of me going home. Although I'm glad to get back home and to see my dear mother again, I'm very sorry not to be able to see you and all my friends in O. before I leave and so I decided to write a few lines to you.

Well, the day which I was waiting for over 3 years, has come now and I'm very glad indeed to get back home, but I'm also very sorry to leave my friends Mr and Mrs Rawcliffe, for we have had a great friendship and please let me thank you that I ever met them and I also like to thank you for all the kindness which my comrades and I have got from you. And when I have got home and I'm looking back to my time in England, I will always remember you and your congregation.

I'm leaving this camp tomorrow and Ashton next Tuesday and I'll let hear from me when I have got home. So I will close now.

Wishing you and your family all the best and may God reward it to you what you have done for us. So

With best wishes,

I'm your sincere and thankful

Heinz Hermann

Heinz had been home only two weeks when he again wrote to my father, from Herne in the British zone:

Herne, 17.10.47

Dear Mr Howe!

I'm sending you and your family the best greetings from my home and I can tell you the glad information that I arrived at home on the 2nd of October. I cannot express what a joy it was when I could see my dear mother and my other family again. They are very glad to have me back.

Well, I found them all in good health. The only one trouble is the food condition, but we have the duty to trust on God

117

and he won't leave us. When I came home I found many things changed. For the first time I didn't know my home again, and I cannot get accustomed to my new civil life. I'm often thinking back of my time in England and always I find a nice memory in it when I'm thinking of you and your congregation. I had to tell my mother and my other family a lot about England and the english people, especially about you and my friends. They all have the only one wish to live in peace with each other.

Hoping that these lines will reach you and your family in the best of health.

I'm remaining
With all the best wishes
Yours sincere and true
   Heinz Hermann
NB Please remember me to Mrs Howe and your children.

In answer to Heinz's Christmas card my father wrote him a letter which received a reply written on 9 February 1948. Here is part of it:

... Well I have got used a bit more to my civilian life, but sometimes it is very hard and I often think back of England, especially Oswaldtwistle. Well, Christmas is now over and I had a nice time and it was grand to be among my family after so long. But I also was thinking of last year which I shall never forget in all my life.

Also the New Year has begun and so let me hope and trust on God that the peace may come to all nations of the world. And then everybody can live in peace with each other. I feel not so well at present, for I got influenza and the weather is terrible at present. What is the weather like in England? ...

Oh, I nearly forgot to tell you that I got a job as a store-man and I like it very well. Well I think I will close and hoping that you and your family are in the best of health when you receive this letter, and God bless.

... I remain with best wishes you sincere friend Also my family send their best wishes.

   Heinz Hermann

A card followed at Easter 1948, and at Christmas 1948 he

wrote again recalling his time in England:

Dear Mr Howe!

I feel a duty to write a few lines to you, as it is only a short time before Christmas. And just at this time my thoughts are going over to your dear congregation and to all my friends in England.

First of all how are you? I hope that you and your family are in the best of health, as I am. Also I can tell you good news, for after one year I got a job in my profession. For I am working as a shop-assistant in a household and tool-shop and I like it very well. The living in Germany today is very dear and so you can think that I am very glad to have a suitable job. My mother always says, when need is greatest God's help is nearest. That has been true this time again.

Last Sunday I went to our friend Bruno Tietze, I think you know him, and we were talking of you all the time, for you see our time in England has been one of the best time of our lives and just this time before Christmas remains a very nice memory for us. How are you going on at Church? I think you are very busy now and I only wish I could be with you all on Christmas Eve, but I shall be in thoughts at Yorkstreet Chapel.

Dear Mr Howe! I wish you a very happy time this Christmas and may God be with you and your Congregation. This is my sincere wish.

Now I'm sending you our very best Christmas-Greetings and God's Bless

I am always you true and sincere friend
    Heinz Hermann

Please give my love to all my friends in Ossy and also my very best Christmas-Greetings.

Although this might have been the last letter written by Herr Hermann to my father, the words in his February letter about Christmas 1946 'which I shall never forget in all my life' have proved to be true. He continued to correspond with the English friends he had made on Christmas day 1946, Mr and Mrs Rawcliffe and their daughter Sheila who sent monthly food parcels until the food situation improved in

Germany.

In August 1973, a generation after the war, Herr Hermann returned to England to visit Sheila, now Mrs Duerden, and her husband. In 1975 he and his wife visited London on a coach tour from Germany, and were able to spend a weekend in Lancashire with Mr and Mrs Duerden. Sheila was particularly pleased to meet Louise Hermann for the first time and says that they laughed and chatted as if they had known each other for a long time even though there was not much common vocabulary between them.

Mr and Mrs Duerden's daughter Susan went to stay with the Hermann family in Germany in September 1973: she was studying O-level German and passed the exam the following year. The two families are still in touch, and in 1990 Herr Hermann described some of his memories in a letter to me:

> ... I still remember you when you were a little girl. And when we left Stanhill Hostel we came with a few men to your house to say your father Good Bye. The time at Stanhill Hostel in 1946 and 1947 has been very nice to us and therefore we have to thank your father, Rev Mr Howe. For he made it possible, that we could get in contact with the Church-People in Oswaldtwistle.
>
> After 26 years, it was in 1973, I came back to England to visit Mrs Sheila Duerden and her husband. We all were very glad to see each other after such a long time. Her parents died before and so I was very sorry I could not see them again. But I met a few old friends again. One Sunday Morning we also visited Stanhill hostel and many happy memories came back.

Mary Clarke (of the Typewriting and Duplicating Bureau) remained good friends with her Christmas Day visitor, Herr Ernst Pensch. She visited him in several camps to which he was moved in England and kept up a correspondence with him when he returned home. She recalls how he used to tell her that they did not want to fight us any more than British citizens wanted to leave home to go to war with Germany.

Mary Clarke became Mrs Jim Clark and Ernst Pensch married Irmgard. One year Mr and Mrs Clark were on their

Fig 34: Mary Clark's reunion with her German friends, September 1987. Left to right: Detlef Pensch, Mary Clark, Irmgard and Ernst Pensch.

way to Germany and intended to visit their friends, but unfortunately Mr Clark was taken ill before leaving England and the trip was cancelled. However, in 1987 after Mary was widowed, she and a friend managed to spend a day with Ernst and Irmgard while on a coach trip in Germany. Their son Detlef was there too. He speaks impeccable English and still acts as translator of letters to this day. Mary writes about the visit in 1987:

> The highlight of the tour was the day we visited Goslar, for it was there I met Ernst and Irmgard and Detlef and Renate (their son and wife). After an exciting tour of the medieval

town of Goslar I was taken to Gros Dohren where Ernst and Irmgard live. I was shown around their Church and introduced to the Minister and his wife, looked around their manse etc. Then after some lovely German meals at Ernst and Irmgard's house where we reminisced about the war years they drove me back to the Panoramic Hotel over the highest part of the Harz Mountains. It was a truly memorable day.

Fred Haworth kept in touch with his Christmas Day visitors, Franz Winschuh and Fritz Herold, and with their friend, Werner Jungnichkel. Franz married, joined the police force and lived in Essen in the British zone. Mr Haworth still has in his possession the photograph of Franz and Leni's wedding, and a photograph of Fritz dated 24 May 1949, sent from his home in East Germany.

There were some German prisoners in Britain who decided after all not to return home to Germany. All prisoners of war who had been held in camps in Britain were repatriated by August 1948 if indeed they wanted to return home. There were, however, a large number, 25,000, who settled in Britain. Several hundred became engaged to local women and by mid-1947 such weddings were permitted.

One of the prisoners in Stanhill camp in 1946, Hans Vallentin, married a local young woman. He had been captured by the Americans off the French coast in 1944, taken to North Africa and then California. Like many of his fellow prisoners he had thought he was on his way home to Germany in 1946 when recrossing the Atlantic, but found his ship docking at Liverpool. He was moved from Stanhill to Merry Thought Camp in Cumberland as a punishment after absconding for a day to visit his girlfriend, Irene. Herr Vallentin's parental home was near Magdeburg in the Russian zone, but he decided not to return and gained permission from the Home Office to stay in Britain. In November 1948 he married Irene and settled down in Oswaldtwistle where he still lives at the time of writing. Mr Vallentin recalls how his mother was glad he had found contentment far from the terrible conditions of post-war Germany.

Many Germans continued to work on farms. Farmers who could provide accommodation could retain ex-prisoners on a civilian basis if their employment was not to the detriment of British workers. Some encountered a little hostility while they were still looked upon as the enemy. However, as Mr Vallentin has said, 'The older people understood what everyone had been through, soldier to soldier'.

It was not in Oswaldtwistle only that deep experiences of friendship led to lasting impressions and the desire to keep in touch after repatriation. One former prisoner, Jürgen Moltmann, held in a camp in Kilmarnock in Scotland, tells 50 years later of his feelings for local people:

In Kilmarnock the miners and their families took us in with a hospitality which shamed us profoundly. We heard no reproaches, we were accused of no guilt. We were accepted as people, even though we were just numbers and wore prisoners' patches on our backs. We experienced forgiveness of guilt without any confession of guilt on our part, and that made it possible for us to live with the past of our people and in the shadow of Auschwitz, without suppression and without becoming callous. I corresponded with the Steele family for a long time.

Dr Moltmann, who also spent time at Norton camp, is now a professor at Tübingen University.

The former prisoner who most faithfully and regularly kept in touch with my own family for two years after his repatriation was of course Heinz Müller. His last full-length letter to my father was written in November 1948, drawing attention to the forthcoming split between the east and the west of Germany:

Leipzig, 19th Nov. 48

Dear Mr Howe,

I definitely believe that you will be convinced that I'm the laziest fellow you ever have known. But it isn't so, by no means. I really tried to write to you several times before, but

123

never succeeded. And then some of your letters came through and I felt at heart that I had to answer as soon as possible. But never could find the time and what is more, couldn't feel like writing letters. I don't know if you will or can understand me.

Life, or better, to make a living was certainly never as hard and difficult as today, and especially in Germany. You may believe me it takes the whole man to get yourself and your family through all these difficulties and hardship of our time. And I'm convinced that there will be no change of the present situation in the near future or even within the next few years. As to the European affair I think there will be a thorough split into an Eastern and a Western part, the former within the Russian influence, the latter within the influence of the Western Powers. Germany will stay split now, split into two halves, which can't live without each other. But it isn't within our power to get a change in the present condition.

In the mean time we grow older and poorer and many of us get hopeless. I'm so glad and so grateful that I managed to bring my family through this time properly. My father and my wife keep good health all the time, and I hope and believe that all of us will do good during the coming winter-time. Until now weather was fine, and even we are in the middle of November it is unusually mild, and the temperature mostly is about 50 degrees F. Right now I caught a cold during my regular business trip. I think I already told you about my journeys, that bring me to Dresden, Berlin, Jena and Rathenow every second week. It always takes me approximately 3 to 4 days to come home again. You may believe me it isn't very comfortable to have to stay at an hotel for one or several nights. Most of the towns will not have one, for you must know Rathenow for example has been destroyed by 63%, Dresden even more, and therefore it will be difficult to find one. If you succeeded and it isn't occupied by the Allied Powers you have to bring along your bed-clothes, the food or at least your meagre ration-card. Trains are still unheated, without windows, or at least without window panes or sometimes with just fragments of panes or fitted with card-boards, in place of panes. There are no light bulbs, I do mean in the train. You can't buy one for your home, either. It isn't very easy to buy anything good and useful now-a-days.

I have to thank you for a few letters, but especially for your picture. We are very glad to have it. Then, there is one more thing I have to thank you. Mrs Peters at Berlin got a wonderful parcel sometime ago from Mrs Foulds, if I'm not mistaken. I'm very grateful that you didn't forget the address I gave you. I answered Mrs Foulds, and translated Mrs Peter's letter. As far as I heard Mrs Foulds promised to send some warm clothes for Donata, Mrs Peters six years old daughter. I think she badly needs warm things, as she is very small and of delicate health, and winter-time will be very very hard for the Berliners this year.

Next month it will be two years since I came home. Everything went well so far, and I have to be thankful. Sometimes I hope and wish to be back in England to see "Mount Pleasant" again and to speak to you about several things, that really matter, but cannot be written.

So, my dear Mr Howe, take mine and my father's and wife's best greetings and wishes for you and your family.

Your good friend
Heinz Müller

The final card from Heinz, dated 18 December 1948, expressed doubts as to whether it would reach its destination and whether my father would ever hear from him again. Were there further letters which never arrived? Did he try to continue the correspondence after Dresden became part of the German Democratic Republic the following year? We shall never know. The last card pays a compliment to my father — generous sentiments with which to move this book towards its end.

Leipzig, Dec 18th 1948

Dear Mr Howe,

I do not know if you will ever get this letter. But anyway I will try it again. The day before yesterday two years before, I came home from England. All of us hoped sincerely for better times to come, but we got badly disappointed. I already told you before, that you will never be able to make yourself a true picture of what life is in Germany today. And I cannot see a change in the future. Oh, no, in the contrary.

But who is to blame?

You will know, even if you shouldn't hear from me again, that our thoughts are very often with you, and that you will be always in my remembrance as one of the finest and most wonderful man I ever met.

Merry Christmas and a happy New-Year to you and your family.

Always your sincere friend

Heinz Müller

My father's five years in Oswaldtwistle came to an end the following year, 1949, and we moved on as usual to our next Methodist circuit. This chapter of our lives closed, but the memories continued in the hearts and minds of people in Germany and England who lived through these moving experiences.

*　　*　　*

The story this book tells has a significance beyond its pages. It is not only a tale of a camp in Oswaldtwistle and resulting friendships between people in Lancashire and Germany. Stories with startling similarities remain largely untold, involving hundreds of other towns and villages in Britain which had prison camps or hostels in their neighbourhoods.

Some recollections are included in two books now only found in certain libraries; *Thresholds of Peace* by Matthew Barry Sullivan, published in 1979, and *Prisoners of England* by Miriam Kochan, published in 1980. Both writers acknowledge that the churches took the lead in helping prisoners who were marooned in Britain at this time. Most of the experiences are still locked in people's memories and likely to die with them. Talk to anyone born before 1930 who attended church regularly in 1946 and you may unearth an untold tale about German prisoners.

Very many Methodist churches, and some Anglican, Baptist, Presbyterian and Roman Catholic churches and Friends Meeting Houses (and probably other denominations too) welcomed prisoners to share in their services. Sermons were preached in English and German, *Stille Nacht* was sung movingly at Christmas, prisoners were invited into private homes once 'fraternisation' was permitted by the government. Music played a therapeutic role and the Society of Friends provided musical instruments for use in camps. Prisoners painstakingly made toys for local children out of scraps of wood and string, and painted crib figures for use in churches at Christmas. Food and clothes parcels were sent to prisoners' families. Prisoners were moved through several camps before at last being allowed to return home. Former prisoners corresponded with their British friends. The impressions these experiences left were deep and lasting. All these factors were the common experiences of thousands of people during 1946 and 1947.

This was an episode in the history of our two countries which gave an initial impetus to the essential process of healing between nations after the Second World War. This view is borne out by a speech made by Rudolf Ahlers in 1995 during the return visit of 29 former German prisoners of Norton camp, the special 'university behind barbed wire' in Nottinghamshire. At a civic reception he stated,

Apart from our studies we will always remember the friendly exchanges with the English people in and around the camp. The winners of the war didn't treat us as defeated persons. They regarded us as human beings; they gave us a new chance in a real Christian manner, to find hope and a purpose in our lives ... So we have all taken the trouble, everybody in his own way, to promote better, more just and democratic conditions at home in our country. This task will never be finished. Because the human heart always tends to laziness, memories are needed to prevent this from happening. This is the purpose of our journey back to England after fifty years.

Those who took part in the numerous but seemingly small acts of friendship can be proud of their part in stimulating reconciliation in Europe. We remember them with gratitude.

Now the remains of the camp at Stanhill are submerged

under tons of concrete supporting a new stretch of motorway. Even so, the memories are not obliterated for those who had the deep satisfaction of seeing for themselves how it is possible for enemies to become real friends.

ENDPIECE

'Mankind is one Great Brotherhood ... We must be resolved to doing all that we can possibly do to avert any future wars.' *Alfred Hindle*

'Therefrom there might develop a true love amongst all nations so we will become one community.' *Walter Schwarz*

'We talked ... of the desire of our people for peace and understanding.' *Joseph H. Howe*

'All people want to live in peace and freedom.' *Heinz Müller*

'Just try to imagine what your own feelings would be in their place.' *Alfred Hindle*

'They all have only one wish to live in peace with each other.' *Heinz Hermann*

'... if men, if nations would understand each other in a better way, things would be better and easier for everybody.' *Heinz Müller*

'... insight into our deep desire to live in peace.' *Joseph H. Howe*

Both sides ' ... have the same simple wish, to live a happy life with their families and to respect the freedom and the individuality of the others.' *Heinz Müller*

'... most sincerely hope that lasting good may be the outcome in many a heart and home.' *Arnold Ashworth*

'And then everybody can live in peace with each other.' *Heinz Hermann*

'A life of golden freedom, the most precious value man is in possession of.' *Heinz Müller*

Fig 35: The author aged nearly seven, and her sister Josey aged twelve, in August 1946 at St Annes on Sea.

INDEX

131